The Kingdom of Rus'

PAST IMPERFECT

Past Imperfect presents concise critical overviews of the latest research by the world's leading scholars. Subjects cross the full range of fields in the period ca. 400—1500 CE which, in a European context, is known as the Middle Ages. Anyone interested in this period will be enthralled and enlightened by these overviews, written in provocative but accessible language. These affordable paperbacks prove that the era still retains a powerful resonance and impact throughout the world today.

Director and Editor-in-Chief

Simon Forde, *Western Michigan University*

Acquisitions Editors

Erin Dailey, *Leeds*
Ruth Kennedy, *Adelaide*

Production

Ruth Kennedy, *Adelaide*

The Kingdom of Rus'

Christian Raffensperger

Library of Congress Cataloging in Publication Data

Names: Raffensperger, Christian, author.

Title: Kingdom of Rus' / by Christian Alexander Raffensperger.

Description: Kalamazoo, MI : Medieval Institute Publications, [2017] |
     Series: Past imprfect | Includes bibliographical references.

Identifiers: LCCN 2017035090 (print) | LCCN 2017035652 (ebook) | ISBN
     9781942401339 | ISBN 9781942401315 (pbk. : alk. paper)

Subjects: LCSH: Kievan Rus--Kings and rulers--History. | Nobility--Kievan
     Rus. | Kievan Rus--Relations--Europe. | Europe--Relations--Kievan Rus.

Classification: LCC DK73 (ebook) | LCC DK73 .R238 2017 (print) | DDC
     947/.02--dc23

LC record available at https://lccn.loc.gov/2017035090

ISBN (print): 9781942401315
eISBN (PDF): 9781942401322
eISBN (EPUB): 9781942401339

arc-humanities.org

Printed and bound by CPI Group (UK) Ltd, Croydon, CR0 4YY

For Iris and Malcolm

Contents

Acknowledgements

Although this is a short book, I have been working on it for a long time in a variety of forms. A lot of people have heard and read pieces of the whole thing and offered their comments. I want to thank all of them, even if I have not singled them out here.

For their feedback on various versions of this project, I would like to thank audiences at the Midwest Medieval Slavic Workshop, the Association for Slavonic, East European, and Eurasian Studies Conference, the Midwest Medieval History Workshop, and the Harvard Early Slavists' Seminar.

I would especially like to thank Francis Butler, who first supported this idea. Whether he agreed with me or not, he was always willing to listen to new ideas and offer supportive encouragement. Similarly, Bill Darden and Don Ostrowski contributed their linguistic and historical expertise to help me attempt to refine some of my ideas; and Elena and Brian Boeck's persistently friendly disagreement helped me to develop my argument.

For the production of the book, I must thank Simon Forde, who conceived of the great idea for this series, and Erin Dailey, who worked with me on developing the proposal and getting it accepted. Both were willing to take me at my word that I could make a translation issue into a readable book and for that I am grateful.

Finally, I want to thank my family, whose support has always been invaluable to me, and especially my children Iris and Malcolm whose intellectual curiosity is consistently motivational to me.

Timeline of Events

This timeline contains events of relevance to Rus', as well as some major events that impact the larger medieval European world, in an attempt to more fully situate Rus' in medieval Europe. It continues from the first Viking explorations in eastern Europe through to the middle of the twelfth century when the picture of Rus' changes. It is selective and meant to illustrate a sampling of events related to the subject of this volume.

793	The first major Viking attack on England, at Lindisfarne.
Late 700s, early 800s	Viking attacks continue throughout western Europe, but raiding also takes place in the Baltic Sea and includes exploration down the Western Dvina and other rivers in eastern Europe.
859–862	The "Povest' vremennykh let" (PVL)—the main source for early Rus'—describes the arrival of the first Rusians in eastern Europe. They come initially as raiders, but then as invited leaders, to the local population. It is more than likely that this is a later justification for rule, given the chronicle's backing by the ruling family, descendants (theoretically) of Riurik.

882	Oleg, also known as Helgi, expands from his base in the north at Novgorod to conquer Kiev, creating the basis for early Rus'.
907	Oleg leads an attack on Constantinople. The attack as described in the PVL is an enormous success and terrifies the Byzantines. The PVL also records the resulting trading treaty, which grants the Rusians numerous trading privileges in Constantinople, testament perhaps to the success of the raid.
941	Igor, known as the son of Riurik, but more likely chronologically a relation of Oleg's, stages another attack on Constantinople. This one does not go as well, and the majority of the Rusian fleet is defeated by the Byzantines using Greek fire. The PVL records a treaty following this attack as well, and this treaty is much more favourable to the Byzantines in its terms.
969–972	Sviatoslav, son of Igor, seeing the opportunities offered by controlling the Balkan trade, "gold, silks, wine, and various fruits from Greece, silver and horses from Hungary and Bohemia, and from Rus' furs wax, honey and slaves" (PVL, s.a. 969), attempts to move his capital to the lower Danube. The Byzantine emperor John Tzimiskes contests this expansion and eventually defeats Sviatoslav in battle, forcing his return to Kiev. On the way to Kiev, Sviatoslav is killed by the nomadic Pechenegs on the River Dnieper, potentially at the behest of the Byzantine emperor.
988/89	Volodimer, son of Sviatoslav, makes an arrangement with Emperor Basil II of Byzantium. Volodimer provides mercenaries for Basil II to put down the simultaneous revolts of Bardas Phokas and Bardas Skleros in exchange for a marriage between Volodimer and Basil II's sister Anna *Porphyrogenita*. Pursuant to Anna and Volodimer's marriage, Volodimer converts to Christianity.

1015	Volodimer, later known as the Christianizer of Rus', dies and there is a struggle over the rule of Rus' within his kinsmen. During the struggle, two of Volodimer's sons, Boris and Gleb, are killed at the bidding of their rival Sviatopolk. Boris and Gleb's non-resistance to their killing leads to their eventual sainthood within Rus'. They become the first two native saints of Rus' and of the ruling dynasty (known alternately as the Riurikids or Volodimerovichi).
1018	Iaroslav the Wise, son of King Volodimer, wins the initial phase of the succession battle and takes up the rule of Kiev. His rule, until 1054, is often known as the Golden Age of Rus'—a time of increasing interconnectivity with the rest of Europe, growing Christianization, the first law code, and many other developments.
1042	Elisabeth, daughter of King Iaroslav, is married to Harald Hardrada. Harald had fled Norway after the defeat of King St. Olaf and found refuge in Rus' with Iaroslav the Wise and his wife Ingigerd. Harald lived and worked in Rus' for some time before going to Constantinople and serving the Byzantine emperor as a member of his Varangian Guard. Eventually leaving Constantinople, he returned to Rus', marrying Elisabeth, and then returning to Norway where, using Elisabeth's familial connections, he claimed the throne of Norway.
1043	Volodimer, eldest son of King Iaroslav, leads a massive attack on the city of Constantinople, the first in one hundred years. Potentially this is in retaliation for an unresolved attack on Rusian merchants.
1043	Iziaslav, son of King Iaroslav, is married to Gertrude, the daughter of Mieszko II and sister of Casimir of Poland. Gertrude would become an important part of Iziaslav's political career, helping to provide aid to him during his two expulsions from rule of Kiev.

1049	Pope Leo IX is chosen as pope. He is the most well known of the German popes and is often considered to be the initiator of what came to be known as the Gregorian Reforms (named after Pope Gregory VII), and thus the Investiture Controversy. He is also associated with the schism of 1054, due to his appointment of Cardinal Humbert to lead a mission to Constantinople, a mission that resulted in the mutual excommunication of pope and patriarch.
1051	Anna, daughter of King Iaroslav (often known as Anna of Kiev), is married to Henry Capet, the ruler of France. Anna becomes an important part of Henry's government, gives birth (and name) to his heir Philip I, and becomes Philip's regent after Henry's death.
1053	Vsevolod, son of King Iaroslav, is married to a daughter of the Monomakhos clan of Byzantium. Potentially this is in relation to a settlement following the Rusian raid on Constantinople in 1043. Vsevolod and the Monomakhina's son, Volodimer will appropriate his mother's familial identity in his name—Volodimer Monomakh.
1054	Iaroslav the Wise dies and power in Kiev passes to his son, Iziaslav. King Iziaslav will rule peacefully for fourteen years.
1066	Harald Hardrada of Norway invades Anglo-Saxon England. He is defeated at Stamford Bridge by King Harold Godwinsson. Harold himself will be beaten later that year at Hastings by Duke William the Bastard of Normandy. Harold's daughter Gyða will end up in Rus' where she marries Volodimer Monomakh, son of Vsevolod Iaroslavich.
1068	King Iziaslav is expelled by the Kievans after a perceived failure to defend them from the nomadic Polovtsy. He seeks refuge in Poland with his kinsman, Bolesław II, who helps him return to rule in Kiev in 1069.

1071	King Iziaslav is expelled a second time. This time he is usurped by his two younger brothers Sviatoslav and Vsevolod. Iziaslav and his family's travels in exile include a stay in Poland and in the German Empire, where Emperor Henry IV sends an emissary to Sviatoslav on his behalf. It also includes the marriage of Iziaslav and Gertrude's son, Iaropolk, to a German noblewoman, Cunigunda. Cunigunda and Iaropolk ultimately were successful in gaining the assistance of Pope Gregory VII, who incentivized Bolesław II to help return Iziaslav to the Kievan throne a second time in 1077.
1071	The Seljuk Turks defeated the Byzantines at the Battle of Manzikert. This battle set the stage for consistent internal conflict within Byzantium and the loss of much of Anatolia for the Byzantines. It is also the catalyst for the eventual rise to power of Alexius Komnenos.
1078	King Iziaslav dies and is succeeded by his only living brother Vsevolod. Vsevolod will rule Rus' until 1093 and will cement his family's power during that time.
1081	Alexius Komnenos seizes the imperial throne in Byzantium. Alexius will rule until 1118. He is not only the progenitor of the Komneni dynasty of emperors, but he is also the father of Anna Komnena (who wrote the *Alexiad* about her father), as well as the emperor who makes the request for assistance that begins the First Crusade.
1089	Evpraksia, daughter of King Vsevolod, is married to Emperor Henry IV of the German Empire. She had initially been married to Margrave Henry III the Long of Stade circa 1082, but he died soon after. This marriage is an attempt to cement an alliance between the German Empire and Rus' to bolster Henry IV's anti-pope Clement III. Clement III actively corresponds with Metropolitan Ioann II of Kiev.

1093	King Vsevolod dies and is succeeded by his nephew, Sviatopolk Iziaslavich. This instance of a peaceful, uncontested succession from uncle to nephew follows the collateral succession model in Rus'.
1095	Evpraksia, daughter of King Vsevolod, speaks at the Papal Synod at Piacenza on behalf of Pope Urban II and against her husband Emperor Henry IV. This helps Urban II win the Investiture Controversy over Henry IV, though an ultimate settlement will not come until early in the next century at the Concordat of Worms. This Papal Synod is also the site for Alexius Komnenos's request for assistance from the papacy that will ultimately transform into the Popular and First Crusades.
1113	King Sviatopolk Iziaslavich dies. He is succeeded by his cousin, Volodimer Monomakh. This is one of the last uncontested and peaceful transitions between families within the larger Volodimerovichi clan within Rus' in the twelfth century. Volodimer himself will institute, or attempt to institute, lineal succession and pass power on to his son, Mstislav/Harald.
1125	King Volodimer Monomakh dies and is succeeded by his son, Mstislav/Harald. Mstislav was also called Harald in Scandinavian sources, attributable to his mother's familial influence. She was Gyða, daughter of Harold Godwinsson, the last Anglo-Saxon king of England.
1138	The death of Bolesław III in Poland leads to the division of Poland amongst his sons. The sons, led by half-brothers Władysław II and Bolesław IV, engage in internal conflict, which helps to hasten splits within Poland, leading to smaller, more autonomous territories after this point.

1146	The death of King Vsevolod Olgovich can be considered to be the end of unity within Rus'. After this time, it is more likely than not that the various rulers of the Rusian cities and regions go in separate directions rather than considering themselves subordinate to the king in Kiev. Primarily this will include Novgorod's increasing ties with the Baltic world of the Hanseatic League; and in the southwest, Galicia-Volhynia's ties are strengthened with Hungary and Poland.
1147	The Second Crusade is called by Pope Eugenius III. The Second Crusade involves not only rulers such as Louis VII of France going to fight in the Crusader states, or attempting to, but also new crusading venues such as Iberia and the Baltic. The creation of crusading in the Baltic against the pagan Wends leads to an expansion of the crusading ideal in which not just Muslims, but now pagans also become the target of crusade.
1150s and 1160s	Iurii Dolgorukii, son of Volodimer Monomakh, and his son, Andrei Bogoliubskii, develop the northeast of Rus' and eventually create their own power centre there, in Vladimir-Suzdal. The creation of a northeastern centre increases the multipolarity of Rus' but also moves one key pole even further from the rest of medieval Europe. The family centred in the northeast will have very few ties with medieval Europe as a whole, but will go on to become the centre of the eventual Muscovite ruling family of Russia.
1159	Henry the Lion, duke of Saxony, rebuilds the port city of Lübeck on the Baltic as a trading city for all of northern Europe. The refoundation of Lübeck will lead to dramatically increased trade in the Baltic, and eventually the creation of the Hanseatic League.

Late 1190s–early 1200s	Rise of crusading in the Baltic. Led by representatives from the Archbishop of Hamburg-Bremen, largely German crusaders begin conquering territory around the Western Dvina River basin, building churches, and spreading Christianity. This expansion of German, Christian power will eventually bring them into conflict with the neighbouring kingdoms of Rus'.
1204	The soldiers of the Fourth Crusade, acting in conjunction with the Venetians, under Doge Enrico Dandolo, sack Constantinople. This event helps to create a further divide between Roman and Orthodox Christianity.
1215	King John is forced to sign the Magna Carta by the English barons as a consequence of his persistent taxation to fund his wars against Philip Augustus of France.
1222	Papal Legate William of Sabina orders non-Roman churches closed in Dorpat on the Baltic. This helps to harden the border between Roman and Orthodox Christianity.
1237/38	The Mongols arrive and attack the Rusian city of Riazan, on the border of the steppe and forest zone. This is the beginning of persistent contact with the Mongols for Rus' and for Christian Europe.
1240	Kiev is sacked by the Mongols. Repercussions are felt throughout Europe, as Kiev was home to people from throughout medieval Europe who communicated about the attack back to their respective places of origin.

1241	The Mongols defeat armies at Mohi and Legnica, destroying a majority of the knighthood of central and eastern Europe from Poland, Bohemia, and Hungary in particular. The death of Khan Ogedei forces a withdrawal of the Mongol armies to the steppe north of the Black Sea. This results in the inclusion of Rus' within the Mongol world empire, and the exclusion of the rest of Europe, thus creating one element of a border between Rus' and the rest of Europe that had not existed earlier.
1240s	A crusade is launched against Rus' and led by both the Swedes and the crusading order known as the Sword Brothers. The crusade of the Swedes was defeated by the ruler of Novgorod, Alexander, and it was where he gained the epithet, Nevsky. He then later defeated the attack of the Sword Brothers at the famous "Battle on the Ice." These events further harden the divide between Roman and Orthodox Christianity, helping to separate Rus' from the rest of medieval Europe.

Introduction

The Problem with Names

For better or for worse, names define concepts, ideas, people, and entities of all sorts. Whether the issue is the title of a medieval ruler or Pluto's designation as a planet, names once given become enshrined in the imagination and become difficult to change, or for those changes to become accepted. There have been many books and journal articles written over the course of hundreds of years that have designated the ruler of Rus' as a "prince" or "duke" and thus the territory he rules as a "principality" or "duchy." On rare occasions, there have been scholars who have differed from this consensus, such as Andrzej Poppe, who used "king" for the ruler of Rus', with the rationale that,

> Since, in early Medieval Europe, the Slavic title *kniaz'* was equivalent to the Latin title *rex*, and since the Rus'ian rulers are constantly referred to in medieval sources as *reges*, I break here with the historiographic tradition of the nineteenth and twentieth centuries and return to the medieval usage and meaning of this title.

But Poppe did not discuss the issue further. Similarly, working on thirteenth-century Galicia (in western Rus'/modern western Ukraine), Mykola Andrusiak made the argument that one of the prominent rulers of Galicia in that time should be called a king.[1] While these rare scholars have bucked the tradition of translating kniaz' as "prince," there has, until now, not been a concerted argument about the use of translation and its relationship to the shaping of the identity of Rus'. Thus, this book will attempt to make what seems like a complex argument: that the ruler of Rus' should be called a king, not a prince; and thus Rus' should be called a kingdom, not a principality.

The process of overturning literally centuries of usage is a difficult one, but this book demonstrates that Rus' of the eleventh and twelfth centuries was not only part of medieval Europe but, in fact, a kingdom. Furthermore, it shows the consequences that making such a seemingly small change will have on our modern interpretation of what medieval Europe looks like. However, making such an enormous change is difficult, and requires stepping through discussion of titles, language, and the study of the Middle Ages. However, at the end, the result will be a newly expanded medieval Europe, without an ahistorical line dividing it into East and West.

Attempting to solve this problem begins with the issue of naming itself—names have power. This concept, that words, names, or labels define ideas, has been explored in academia in recent decades under the label, "the linguistic turn." The linguistic turn has influenced nearly all of academia and caused a reevaluation of the way academics articulate ideas. Even more, that reevaluation has caused a rethinking of the basic constructs that academics are working with as their building blocks: words. It is very important for our study of history to understand that concepts are often created and apply to a specific place and time; and then to apply them accurately and appropriately and not over-broadly.

Applying this concept starts with "Rus'," the name of the medieval polity under discussion. Rus' occupied part of the territory of three modern states—Russia, Ukraine, and Belarus. This situation has caused historical confusion when dealing with the name of this medieval territory. For some, such as nationalist historians of Ukraine and Russia, claiming the name of Rus' as their exclusive heritage creates historical legitimacy for their preferred government to rule the territory of the Dnieper River valley, which was the heartland of medieval Rus'. (This is certainly apparent in the current appropriation of the history of Rus' by Vladimir Putin in his campaign to claim territory from Ukraine.) For others, even medieval scholars, it is simply an issue of lack of knowledge of the appropriate medieval terminology. The name "Russia" is a known quantity and thus ends up as a label on maps covering both the medieval and modern periods. For still others, there is the issue of convenience (even when they know better). Rus' is a label that requires an explanation. It even has an odd diacritic at the end that some, but not all, scholars use in English to represent an Old East Slavic character (a "soft sign") that does not exist in English. Even more confusingly, the adjectival form of Rus' is "Rusian," which most people, and most spell-check software, want to convert to "Russian." Thus proper historical terminology can be difficult to use when talking with a broad audience. Moreover, it does not serve as a label well beyond the medieval period. The political situation of Rus' becomes increasingly complex over the thirteenth century and begins to splinter into multiple polities over the course of that period and into the fourteenth century as well. Thus, for any class or book, textbook for example, that crosses over that period, Rus' is a difficult label to use. For my own purposes, I have used "Medieval Russia" as a label for the class that I teach about Rus', because it extends into the period of the rise of Muscovy, and it fits into a broader sequence of classes in the Russian and Central Eurasian Studies Program that includes "Imperial Russia" and "Soviet Russia." And yet, despite all those reasons for not using "Rus'," it is the temporally correct name for the medieval polity based at Kiev on the River Dnieper. Using it also allows us to sidestep a nationalist quagmire. But it does, admittedly, require an explanation.

Medieval names, as well as modern ones, are problematic creations that carry with them a variety of cultural baggage, and have been used (and misused) to delineate various groups and leaders. Medieval titles carry the same problem, especially when translated into another language with cultural baggage knowingly or unknowingly attached, as Florin Curta has also discussed in regard to the medieval Balkans.[2] To understand how Rus' is a kingdom, we need to start with an understanding of the titles of rulers—titulature. There are a variety of medieval European titles that have been translated into modern English as "king": *rex* (Latin), *konungr* (Old Norse), *cyning* (Anglo-Saxon), *rí* (Irish), and even occasionally *kniaz'* (Old East Slavic). These titles all had the root meaning of leader, and gained additional meanings or levels of meaning over time. The basic purpose of this book is to, through an investigation of titulature, demonstrate that Rus' was a kingdom. In so doing, I hope to point out some of the problems inherent in the modern, often unthinking use of titles, both in regard to Rus' and elsewhere in Europe. For example, Anglo-Saxon rulers, both before and after Charlemagne's imperial coronation in 800 (d. 814), claimed the imperial title themselves. They styled themselves *Basileus Anglorum* (emperor of the Angles) in a self-conscious appropriation of Byzantine titulature.[3] Both for Charlemagne on the continent and these rulers in England, they chose to use a Roman imperial title (*imperator* or *basileus*—both of which are translated typically as "emperor") to connect themselves to their shared Roman imperial past, as a way of appropriating some of that grandeur and legitimacy. However, if we then look at modern scholarship on these rulers who claimed the imperial title, it is only Charlemagne who is given the title of "emperor" in English, sometimes "emperor of the Romans," more often "emperor of the Franks." The Anglo-Saxon rulers who used the imperial title are never referred to in English as "emperor of the Angles"; they are almost always called kings of whatever region they rule. Anders Winroth puts together a sentence that encapsulates the problems of titulature, including this example, quite beautifully: "In the eyes of Scandinavian chieftains aspiring to power, the religion of Emperor Charlemagne, the emperor in Constantinople, and the kings in the British Isles must have been a fine religion indeed."[4] Similarly, but in a slightly later period, the Ottonians and Salians ruled a territory that has been referred to anachronistically as the Holy Roman Empire, territorially as the German Empire, or simply as the *Reich* (Leyser, p. 216). The title that they used for themselves was much more often *rex* or *imperator Romanorum* (emperor of the Romans), rarely *Teutonicorum* (of the Teutons/Germans), but they are not referred to as Roman kings, or emperors, in secondary sources.[5]

The same situation is true for labels other than titles, even amongst specialists. The nearly universal formulation for the Eastern Roman Empire centred at Constantinople, especially after the fifth century, is Byzantium or the Byzantine Empire. This creates in the mind of the reader a certain picture, entirely different from that created by the names "Rome" or "Roman," which was the point of the creation of the concept. However, for the medieval people about whom we are writing, utilizing the concept of Byzantium is problematic, as none of them would have understood the term; all would have conceptualized of it as Rome, at least in some particulars, even if they did not like it. Our modern use of names can create a barrier to our perception of history and requires us, and our audience, to perform mental gymnastics each time we use the concept to keep in mind what "Byzantium" was, to whom, and when.

Combining these mental gymnastics with the shifting labels between medieval and modern titulature leads to the potential for confusion in our modern understanding of medieval history. To attempt to clarify this situation, this book offers instead the idea that there were no dukes or princes of Rus' in the eleventh and twelfth centuries; instead, there were kings. At its root, this argument is not all that complex—the chapters here will progress through a series of interconnected ideas to develop the argument. The first chapter lays out the background for the situation, including the traditional view of medieval Europe, and why Rus' should even be considered as part of medieval Europe. From there, chapter 2 looks back at how the translation of kniaz as "prince" was established. Much like the conception of medieval Europe seen in chapter 1, it is an evolutionary process that starts with good ideas and then becomes stuck in the past, not evolving with new ideas or understandings. Chapter 3 moves into discussion of the titles for medieval rulers in general, including the problems with how those titles are applied. Chapter 4 addresses the issue of what was a kniaz', this title for a medieval Rusian ruler—what did they do, what were their functions? This flows into the next two chapters, which deal respectively with what titles medieval sources used for these Rusian rulers, and what titles Rusian sources used for their own and other rulers. All this combines to establish a baseline understanding of the rulers, their functions, and how they are referred to throughout medieval Europe. Finally, in the conclusion, we come back to one of the basic questions that historians ask, and which should be asked of historians: "So what?" The impact and consequences of making a kingdom of Rus' are seen in a couple of small examples that demonstrate the impact of even small changes on our perception and understanding of the past. All of this combines to articulate the larger idea that we need to not just include eastern Europe in medieval Europe, but to utilize proper terminology for medieval European polities. In the case of Rus', this creates the largest European kingdom of the eleventh and twelfth century—the kingdom of Rus'.

Notes

[1] Andrzej Poppe, "The Sainthood of Vladimir the Great: Veneration in the Making," in *Christian Russia in the Making* (Aldershot: Ashgate, 2007); Mykola Andrusiak and A. Mykytiak, "Kings of Kiev and Galicia: On the Occassion of the 700th Anniversary of the Coronation of Danilo Romanovich," *Slavonic and East European Review* 33 (1955): 342–49.

[2] Florin Curta, "Qagan, Khan, or King? Power in Early Medieval Bulgaria (Seventh to Ninth Centuries)," *Viator* 37 (2006): 1–31.

[3] Peter Brown, *The Rise of Western Christendom: Triumph and Diversity, A.D. 200–1000*, 2nd ed. (Malden: Blackwell, 2003), p. 477; Walter de Gray Birch lists all of the titles claimed by Anglo-Saxon and Norman kings, including *"Anglorum basileus"* in his, "Index of the Styles and Titles of English Sovereigns," in *Report of the First Annual Meeting of the Index Society* (London, 1879), pp. 52–53.

[4] *The Conversion of Scandinavia: Vikings, Merchants, and Missionaries in the Remaking of Northern Europe* (New Haven: Yale University Press, 2012), p. 140.

[5] Otto III and Henry IV were both crowned as emperors, as was Henry III, and all were crowned as *imperator Romanorum*. There is a good deal of literature on this subject, but Gerd Althoff and I. S. Robinson cover the topic well for our purposes. Gerd Althoff, *Otto III*, trans. Phyllis G. Jestice (University Park: Pennsylvania State University Press, 2003), pp. 83–97; I. S. Robinson, *Henry IV of Germany, 1056–1106* (Cambridge: Cambridge University Press, 1999), pp. 230–31.

Chapter I

The Place of Rus' in Europe

Europe is a place. It is a continent, though with only impre-
cise divisions from Asia, and one that schoolchildren are
required to learn about as part of elementary geography
lessons. Europe is also an idea. This can be seen most
clearly in the expansion, and contraction, of the European
Union (EU). Is Ukraine "European" enough for membership
in the EU, as was discussed in the early 2010s? Or is Britain
becoming *too* European and thus needing to leave the EU,
as the Brexit (British Exit) campaign suggested in the
mid-2010s? For our hypothetical schoolchild learning their
geography, both Ukraine and Britain are included within
the boundary of Europe. However, in many minds, the question remains: are they part of the idea of Europe?

Traditional Medieval Europe

This same quandary pertains to medieval Europe. In fact,
because it is in the past, it perhaps pertains even more,
as we can only impose our ideas upon it and it cannot argue
back. We can make the same distinction for medieval Europe
regarding geography versus idea, but even there, we run
into problems: the geography of Europe (or at least the
conceptualization of territory in the medieval mind) is still
being defined in the medieval period and so we are forced

further into the realm of ideas. The idea of medieval Europe, the one that is on the minds of non-specialists as well as most specialists, is one of castles, knights, princesses, dragons (yes, mostly non-specialists, but not all ...). It is best represented by England, France, and the papacy, and does not really include very much else. The Vikings were outsiders attacking England, France, and the papacy. The crusades were England, France, and the papacy acting upon the Islamic world. The main events were the rise of Charlemagne (France is great); the Normans (from France) taking over England; King John signing the Magna Carta; the wars of Philip Augustus of France and King John for control over continental (French) territory; the wars of the various Edwards of England with Scotland (and France); the Hundred Years' War between England and France; and maybe the Great Schism, where there were two (at least) popes (who were usually backed by England and France). This may not be the exact curriculum offered, but it would enable most non-specialists to get by with a passing grade in medieval European history.

The picture of medieval Europe that I have painted here is a slightly exaggerated one from the normative picture presented by many medieval historians and their textbooks. The maps in those books often end at the River Rhine, as if there was nothing to the east to be found. (I suppose it is fortunate that the mapmakers at least chose to forsake adding dragons in that territory and just left it blank.) Though not a textbook, the magisterial *Framing the Early Middle Ages* by Chris Wickham needs mention here. It creates a new idea of the Middle Ages, outside traditional, national boundaries of western Europe. It includes traditional western Europe, but also Iberia, north Africa, Egypt, the eastern Mediterranean, and Byzantium. However, it specifically does not include the Slavic world. Despite this work, the traditional idea of medieval Europe is a common one and was created slowly over time, so slowly that it seems as if it has always been that way. Historians have looked at the creation of the idea of Eastern Europe, the idea of Byzantium, and the growth of similar ideas. What seems to be the case is that those ideas are largely a function of the early modern past. This is not the place to get into the specifics of those ideas, but suffice it to say that the idea of medieval Europe about which I am speaking did not spring forth fully grown from the collective minds of modern historians. It has gestated slowly through many minds and many histories over many years. It has also had a great deal of momentum added to it over that time due to various political developments that seemed to create differences in the European experience. Just a sampling would include the fairly early ideas of nation-state created in England and France, as opposed to the multiplicity of German and Italian polities; the growth of multinational continental empires of Germany, Austria–Hungary, and Russia, as opposed to the expansion to the Western Hemisphere of England, France, and Spain; or even the relatively recent Cold War division in Europe between democratic and communist states. They all helped build a mindset that the idea of Europe pertained to England and France, and perhaps some near neighbours, but not to everyone on the continent of Europe. It was a small step then to read that idea of Europe back into the medieval past, especially as the medieval past was seen as a tool to create modern legitimacy.

This mindset is inherently limiting, especially when historians are discussing the past. Yes, England, France, and the papacy were medieval Europe, but so were others; and those others were also actors, creating effects that resonated near and far, sometimes even affecting England and France. Imagining a medieval Europe without those people, places, religions, ideas, and so on created an inaccurate sense of self-knowledge, as historians felt that they understood the actions and actors who populated their medieval Europe.

One of the most famous examples of this is the debate about feudalism. Through the nineteenth and early twentieth centuries, feudalism was an emblematic idea of the Middle Ages. However, in the last decades of the twentieth century, historians such as Elizabeth Brown and Susan Reynolds pointed out that the creation of the idea of feudalism hinged on late medieval French documents, and that it did not map to the majority of western Europe in the way that had been described for so long (not to mention the rest of Europe, of course). (See Richard Abel's overview of the debate and its history.) This revision to the understanding of feudalism caused a wave of reimagining both social and economic structures in regard to medieval western Europe. In the early twenty-first century, a further challenge emerged suggesting that feudalism may still be a valid term of discourse with a particular set of definitions. Some of those scholars, such as Yulia Mikhailova, used evidence not from western Europe, but from eastern Europe. The addition of new territory and new evidence changed the discussion, and added to the evidentiary base. Returning to Chris Wickham's broad new formulation of Europe, he suggested that medievalists often focus tightly in on one area, to the exclusion of the larger picture. Admittedly, including all of medieval Europe is a tall order, but the inclusion of a wider range of territory leads to a wider range of evidence, and thus we can construct a more accurate picture of medieval life.

Where this all leaves us is with the current description of medieval Europe being limited and inadequate. Instead of encompassing all of the continent of Europe, or the territory of Christian Europe, it traditionally only addresses a small subset of that territory. A better understanding of

the history, processes, and above all the breadth of medieval Europe can be gained by looking at medieval Europe
in its entirety.

Rus' as Part of Medieval Europe

As the title of this section intimates, the medieval Europe
discussed here will be larger than the one addressed above,
which could be referred to as the traditional perspective.
(To their credit and to be fair, professional medieval historians acknowledge this, but they do continue to focus
on what they know best, a common enough problem.) As
this book has the kingdom of Rus' as its particular focus,
that is the piece of Europe that I will add in here; however, it should be understood that similar arguments could
be, and have been, made for Hungary, Poland, and so on.
What I would like to provide here is a basic primer for the
interconnectivity of the kingdom of Rus' with the rest of
medieval Europe.[6] Ideally, through an examination of the
marital and religious ties, a picture will be created that
shows that Rus' was part and parcel of medieval Europe.
This will lay the foundation for the larger discussion of the
book regarding the title of the ruler of Rus', the title of the
polity, and the challenges and relevance of such questions
for medieval Europe as a whole.

Dynastic Marriage

One of the easiest ways to demonstrate that Rus' was
part of medieval Europe is to look at actual, physical connections between Rus' and the rest of medieval Europe.
Royal families, as is well known from more modern history, are deeply interconnected and medieval Europe was
the beginning of this interconnectivity. I will outline three
examples of dynastic, royal marriages between Rusian
princesses and royals from the rest of Europe. These

three marriages are just examples of a much larger set of marriages connecting Rus' with the rest of Europe (see Raffensperger, *Ties of Kinship*). It should be remembered that marriages at this elite level were not just the union of one man and one woman; they were negotiated by emissaries, often high ecclesiastics. The ceremonies were grand spectacles. The bride brought with her not only a dowry, but an entourage of people who spoke her language and worked as assistants, advocates, and guards, as well as carrying out many other duties. In effect, each of these marriages is a diplomatic embassy right in the very bed-chamber of a foreign ruler.

Agafia, also called Agatha, was the daughter of Iaroslav the Wise (d. 1054), one of the greatest rulers of Rus' in the middle of the eleventh century. Agafia was, most likely, his eldest daughter and potentially the first to get married. Part of what led to Iaroslav's fame and greatness was his propensity for giving sanctuary to royals, especially children, exiled from their homelands for one reason or another. While they were living at his court, Iaroslav also often arranged marriages for these exiles with his family members. This was obviously a gamble, but if the exiled royal prince were to return to his homeland and rule, one of Iaroslav's daughters would be his queen.

The case of Agafia began in this way, as did so many others. In the early eleventh century, Cnut the Great (d. 1035) took power in England and exiled the previous ruler's sons, Edmund and Edward. After a circuitous journey, those exiled princes ended up in Rus' at the court of Iaroslav. Iaroslav gave them a home, and married his daughter Agafia to Edward, who is known in modern scholarship as Edward the Exile. Edward and Agafia left Rus' in company with Agafia's sister Anastasia and her husband Andrew (d. 1060). Andrew, a fellow exile in Rus', was returning to Hungary to take his place on the throne. In

1054, Edward the Exile and Agafia were summoned to England by King Edward the Confessor (d. 1066), who was hoping that Edward would be his heir and continue the line of kings of Wessex that was interrupted by Cnut and restored by Edward the Confessor. Unfortunately, upon Edward the Exile's arrival in England in 1057 he died under mysterious circumstances. Newly widowed, Agafia travelled to Scotland, where she made a home for her family and arranged the marriage of her daughter Margaret with the Scottish king Malcolm III (d. 1093).

Though the marriage may not have served Iaroslav's initial purpose of having his daughter become queen of England, it almost worked. And for our purposes it provides evidence of the deeper interconnectivity of Rus' with one of the stalwarts of traditional medieval Europe—England. Agafia did marry the English prince, they did have children, and those children continued the tradition of dynastic marriage, such that Iaroslav's granddaughter became queen of Scotland (later, his great-granddaughter, daughter of Margaret and Malcolm III, did become queen of England). In fact, Agafia's son, Iaroslav's grandson, Edgar Aethling (Prince Edgar) fought against William the Conqueror (d. 1087) after 1066, and allied with his half-Rusian cousin King Philip of France (d. 1108) to do so.

Much like the example of Agafia above, Cnut the Great is responsible (indirectly) for this marriage as well. In 1030, the forces of King Cnut defeated King (later St.) Olaf of Norway (d. 1030), and multiple partisans of Olaf fled Norway, including Olaf's younger brother Harald. Harald travelled east to Rus', where he took refuge with Iaroslav, and with Iaroslav's wife Ingigerd, who was a Swedish princess and whose sister was married to King St. Olaf. Harald did not stay long in Rus', but he seems to have developed a relationship with one of Iaroslav's daughters during that time—later identified as Elisabeth.

Harald next travelled to Byzantium, where he served in the emperor's Varangian Guard and distinguished himself in multiple campaigns, sending money home to Iaroslav's court to keep it safe. Eventually, he too returned to Rus', which a Scandinavian skaldic poem recorded in the *Heim-skringla* tells us was motivated by his love for a Rusian woman. Back in Rus', he married Elisabeth and promptly left for Scandinavia to attempt to claim the Norwegian throne, or a share of it, from the current ruler, his nephew Magnus (d. 1047). Elisabeth went with him, and was a key part of his attempt, as when they arrived in Scandinavia he used her familial connections (claiming her kinship ties as his own) to build relationships with other rulers, including King Sven Estridsson of Denmark (d. ca. 1076). These ties, as well as his own with Magnus, cemented his success and he claimed part of the rule of Norway. Elisabeth often travelled with her husband, even after having children, and she went along on the fateful voyage in 1066 that saw Harald, by then called Hardrada, killed during his assault on the north of England.

Elisabeth's marriage was another in the line of gambles that Iaroslav the Wise took with the marital fortunes of his children, but it certainly worked out. His daughter married one of the most well-known Scandinavian kings in Europe, one who fought in Rus', Byzantium, Scandinavia, and England, and came close to conquering the latter. She would not be the last Rusian woman to marry into a Scandinavian royal family.

The final union I would like to discuss actually concerns two dynastic marriages. This discussion will serve as an introduction to the next section on religious interconnectivity as well. Evpraksia was the daughter of Vsevolod Iaroslavich, ruler of Rus' from 1078 to 1093. One of the goals of Iaroslav, Vsevolod's father, had been to create a marital tie with the powerful German Empire. However, despite his success in making marriages between his family and Byzantium, England, France, Hungary, Poland, and Norway, he had not been able to build a connection with the German Empire. It was not until the rule of Vsevolod that the conditions were right to make such a marital alliance happen. In the early 1080s, Henry IV, the German emperor (d. 1106), was in a struggle with the papacy known as the Investiture Controversy (which will be discussed more in the next section). As part of that conflict, an alliance with Rus' was deemed desirable and Henry IV and Vsevolod arranged the marriage of Evpraksia with one of Henry's subjects, also named Henry: Henry III the Long, margrave of the Saxon Nordmark (d. 1087). Henry IV himself was still married at this time, and thus he was unavailable for a marriage alliance. In addition, Henry III the Long was much closer in age to the teenage Evpraksia, making the pairing seem a kinder choice. Evpraksia's arrival in the German Empire was noted for its opulence and for the enormous baggage train she brought with her from Rus', indicative of the large entourage as well.

Soon after the marriage of Evpraksia and Henry III the Long, Henry died. Childless and thus with no tie or claim to her husband's territory, Evpraksia did not stay single long; Emperor Henry IV's wife died soon after, and so he and Evpraksia were married. In 1089, Evpraksia was crowned Empress of the German Empire. This marriage was not to be a success, but at the moment of the marriage it was clear that Evpraksia was the highest placed and most visible Rusian woman in the medieval world. (This is especially true as the queens of Rus' were often from other places—Iaroslav's wife was from Sweden, Vsevolod's from Byzantium.) The marriage was also part of Henry IV's attempt to build alliances with Rus', related to the Investiture Controversy; the demise of the marriage is related to that controversy as well. Only a few years into the marriage, Evpraksia left her husband and began to speak out against him, in favour of Pope Urban II (d. 1099), Henry IV's opponent. Evpraksia spoke at multiple gatherings of bishops and finally at the papal council of Piacenza in 1095. At each gathering she spoke about her ill treatment at Henry IV's hands, and about the goodness and holiness of the pope (all stories written for her by papal propagandists).

The denouement of Evpraksia's life found her in a nunnery in Rus' where she eventually died in 1109 and was honoured with a burial in the most holy place in Rus'. Though her marriage did not work out the way that Henry IV and Vsevolod may have originally intended, it certainly elevated the position of Rus' on the medieval European stage, and cemented her as an actor on behalf of her family and Rus' in general.

These marriages taken together demonstrate the interconnectivity of the Rusian royal family (referred to by scholars either as the Volodimerovichi or Riurikids) with the other royal families of medieval Europe.[7] Women were the warp and weft of those connections, weaving medieval Europe's royal families into one large, interconnected tapestry of kinship relations.

Medieval Christianities

One of the defining features of medieval Europe is the power of the Christian Church. However, the image of an all-powerful medieval church is not an entirely accurate one, certainly not for the eleventh century, nor is the image of a Catholic Church split from the Orthodox Church. Certainly before 1204, there may have been disagreements between the patriarch of Constantinople and the pope in Rome, but the respective churches and their worshipers were largely in communion with one another. For our purposes, what this means is that Rus' was not aligned with Byzantium and the Orthodox Church and thus was opposed to Rome and the Roman/Catholic Church. They were all part of one larger Christian world worshipping the same god by the same, general, rites and rituals. In discussing this, I will lay out three examples of religious interactions involving Rus' and the papacy, beginning with the Christianization of Rus', continuing with one particular church commemoration, and concluding with the Investiture Controversy mentioned above.

In 988 or 989, Volodimer, the ruler of Rus' (d. 1015), converted to Christianity in order to marry Anna *Porphyrogenita*, daughter of one Byzantine emperor and sister to two others. Volodimer was baptized in Cherson, a city on the Black Sea, by the bishop. When he returned to Kiev with Anna, he ordered the people of that city baptized as well. This is the story, in brief, of the conversion of Rus'. The ecclesiastical establishment of Rus' grew slowly from this point, and ecclesiastical officials from Byzantium eventually became dominant, headed by metropolitans (an office similar to archbishop) located in Kiev. However, from the very beginning of Rusian Christianity, there were strong ties with the papacy as well.

While Volodimer was besieging the city of Cherson, prior to his baptism, he received an emissary from the papacy bringing him the relics of St. Clement. These were particularly potent relics of a famous, sainted, early pope. This early bishop of Rome had been exiled to the Black Sea and died there, his relics only recovered centuries later by Constantine, later known as St. Cyril (often called the Apostle to the Slavs, as he was responsible for creating an alphabet for the Slavic language). The return of those relics to the Black Sea region, as a gift to this newly Christianized ruler, were meant to show the generosity of the papacy as well as to perhaps woo Volodimer into a closer connection with the papacy. The relics remained in Rus', and became a prominent part of the Rusian Church. More embassies flowed back and forth with Rome, but nothing more seems to have come of this relationship in the late tenth century.

Those tenth-century embassies were not the end of contact between the papacy and Rus', however. Another important interaction occurred at the end of the eleventh century when a group of Italian merchants "liberated" the relics of St. Nicholas from Myra and took them to Bari in the south of the Italian peninsula. This was celebrated in Rome with the pope, Urban II, writing a new celebration for the Feast of the Translation of the Relics of St. Nicholas, which was to be celebrated on May 9. This celebration, however, was an affront to the Byzantines. It was from them that the relics were liberated as the merchants worried, purportedly, that they were unsafe in such close proximity to Islamic territory. Thus, Pope Urban II's celebratory feast, its text, and resulting yearly celebration were never incorporated into the Byzantine Church calendar.

This was not the case, however, in Rus'. This feast does occur in the Rusian Church calendar and was celebrated yearly on May 9, the same as throughout the Roman Christian world. It was most likely introduced into Rus' by a visit of a papal embassy in 1091, continuing the relationship between the two sides. This visit, too, was said to be one in which the papal emissaries brought relics for Rus'. Though the metropolitan of Rus' reported to the patriarch in Constantinople rather than the pope in Rome, the Rusian Church still enjoyed good relations with the papacy, including adopting holidays which, at least in some ways, were antithetical to the Byzantine, "Orthodox" Church. Such connections are representative of the place of Rus' within a larger, shared, Christian European world.

The last example of religious interconnectivity between Rus' and the rest of medieval Europe comes from an incident already mentioned in regard to the marriage of

Henry IV and Evpraksia Vsevolodovna: the Investiture Controversy. This controversy centred on the question of who had the power to grant authority to ecclesiastical officials—the pope or secular rulers. Pope Gregory VII (d. 1085) began the controversy (and the growth of papal power) by excommunicating Henry IV for his continued appointment of ecclesiastical officials. This controversy, begun in the 1070s, continued through multiple successors until the early twelfth century. The piece that we are interested in concerns Henry IV's attempt to bring Rus' into the struggle, on his side, and the failure of that attempt.

In his quest to overthrow Pope Gregory VII, Henry IV named his own pope, Clement III (d. 1100) (traditionally referred to as an anti-pope). Clement III had the support of much of the German Empire, as well as elsewhere, and wrote to the metropolitan of Rus', in Kiev, for the support of the Rusian Church as well (a move taken in parallel with Henry IV's dynastic marriage negotiations with Vsevolod, the ruler of Rus'). Though the metropolitan rebuffed Clement III's advances, the attempt was important because it demonstrated that Rus' was another area—among many others such as France, Poland, and England—that the anti-pope attempted to sway to his side; he did not view it as untouchable or as part of another sphere of influence entirely.

This, however, is not the end of the story. When Evpraksia left her husband, Henry IV, she did so to side with the papacy against him. She travelled around Europe, speaking to gatherings of bishops, telling them about her husband's sins and about the greatness of the pope (by this time Urban II). Evpraksia's shift in loyalties helped to sway the Investiture Controversy into the hands of the papacy. This is especially true if it is accepted that she was also responsible for bringing over one of Henry IV's sons, by his first marriage, to the papal side as well.

If we were to imagine the traditional medieval Europe that does not include Rus', this story would never happen. But it did. And not only that, Evpraksia, who was empress of the German Empire and spoke on behalf of the Roman pope, was not shunned at home for allying herself with the Roman Christian world and its spiritual leader; instead she ended her life in Rus' as a nun, after her husband Henry IV's death, and at her death she was given a burial in the holiest place possible in Rus', as well as multiple mentions in the Rusian sources, which are largely reserved for men. All of this indicates that there was no religious animus regarding her time in the west, with either Henry IV or Pope Urban II; rather, she was honoured with a prestigious burial for her work representing Rus' and her family.

These few examples demonstrate the deep religious inter-connectivity throughout Europe, specifically between Rus' and the papacy. These ties are largely omitted from traditional histories and thus not only is Rus' left out, but so are large pieces of what might be going on in each of these situations. The Investiture Controversy is the most potent example, as it is told throughout textbooks on medieval history and yet Rus' never gets a mention, despite the enormous role played by Evpraksia. Incorporating Rus', and elsewhere, is an essential component to understanding what medieval Europe was, what happened there, and why.

Rus' was part of medieval Europe, even beyond the religious and marital connections illustrated here. The dominant trade routes in which they participated were with Byzantium to the south and Scandinavia to the north; Poland, Hungary, and the German Empire to the west; and of particular importance moving into the twelfth century was trade on the Baltic Sea. Rus' also shared craftsmen and artisans with multiple Italian cities, most popularly mosaicists originating from the Byzantine Empire. They even used architects from the German Empire to build some of the churches in their new regions near the River Volga. The connections delineated here are just the tip of the iceberg in regard to building a picture of a larger medieval Europe, but ideally it will suffice as an introduction to this new vision of a new Europe.

A Better Look at Europe

Having built a larger medieval Europe, at least in outline form, we can see that it is a much different world from what is traditionally perceived as "medieval Europe." Hopefully, it is equally clear why building this larger medieval Europe is so important. Taking the Investiture Controversy as an example, we can see how including Rus', specifically Rusian politics and people, in the analysis of this controversy helps to tell a larger, more interesting and more accurate story. It is not just a story of the German Empire and the papacy, but one that includes nearly all of Europe—west and east.

The remainder of this book takes this a step further, looking at one specific example: titles. Titles are important indicators of status. In particular, when multiple individuals are listed together, title is a way to rank them and delineate who is the most powerful among friends, enemies, allies, and neighbours. The title of the ruler of Rus' is no different and therefore no less important. Thus, with Rus' firmly established in Europe, we can proceed to an examination of the titles of the Rusian leaders in their proper context—that of medieval Europe as a whole.

Notes

[6] For a more in-depth examination of these issues, please see Christian Raffensperger, *Reimagining Europe: Kievan Rus' in the Medieval World* (Cambridge, MA: Harvard University Press, 2012).

[7] I prefer the term "Volodimerovichi" for the family ruling Rus' in this period because I believe it is more accurate than the more commonly used "Riurikids." Riurik was the mythical progenitor of the ruling family and not claimed as an honoured descendant until well after this period. Volodimer Sviatoslavich, on the other hand, was the Christianizer of Rus' in the late tenth century and the ruler back to which all subsequent kniazia attempted to trace their descent. Thus, I refer to those kniazia as the children of Volodimer, the Volodimerovichi. For more on this change in naming see Donald Ostrowski, "Systems of Succession in Rus' and Steppe Societies," *Ruthenica* 11 (2012): 29–58.

Chapter 2

The Historiography of the Translation of Kniaz'

The current translation of kniaz' into English as "prince" or "duke" did not arise in a vacuum. Translations, like historical documents themselves, are products of their time and of their translator. As we delve into the issue of the translation of this title, it is important to understand where the impetus to translate kniaz' into English as "duke" or "prince" came from, to better appreciate why it was translated that way and to learn how to correct it. We must also note two additional, complicating factors: the first is the prevalence of this title and its use in modern secondary sources—this helps us properly appreciate the scale of the task of changing the translation of this one word; the second is the fact that the translation of kniaz' as "prince" or "duke" is correct for certain historical periods, just not for the period under discussion.

Historical Background to Translation

In the middle of the sixteenth century, British merchants seeking a faster way to reach central and south Asia began crossing through the eastern European river systems, and increasing their dealings with the Muscovite (or Russian in some secondary sources) ruler. What they found was a government led by a tsar', surrounded by a series of other members of his family who helped him govern, the majority of whom bore the title "kniaz'." Giles Fletcher's "Of the Russe Commonwealth" is one of the most comprehensive descriptions of Muscovy in this period by an English traveller and will stand in as an example of the genre. He describes the Muscovite government, tsar', and ruling families in some detail. Of the kniazia (plural for kniaz', and a term he uses) he says, "The fourth and lowest degree of nobility with them is of such as bear the name of kniaz'ia or dukes but come of the younger brothers of those chief houses through many descents and have no inheritance of their own, save the bare name or title of duke only." He continues in this vein using "duke" and "kniaz'" interchangeably.[8] This change in power structure from the period we are interested in until the arrival of the English in Muscovy was the result of increasing centralization over the fourteenth century, and the practical subordination of most of the Volodimerovichi to a few individuals, such as the ruler of Moscow (see, for example, Kollman, pp. 46–47). That subordination resulted in a similar change in the use of titulature to what was seen earlier in western Europe, with the result that males born into the Volodimerovichi family all carried the title "kniaz'," even if they had no city, office, or practical power. In the eyes of the English merchants and others travelling through Muscovy it was clear that the tsar' was paramount and the kniazia were secondary, or even lower in rank, officials, though largely of the same family. Thus, they typically translated kniaz' as "duke," fitting it into their own English conception of hierarchies of noble rank. This translation was reasonable at the time, and for many centuries after.[9] The translation of kniaz' shifted slightly from "duke" to "prince" in the twentieth century, perhaps as a way of removing links between the recently overthrown imperial past and the more remote medieval era, though this is just speculation.

Regardless of rationale, the majority of modern English-language publications discussing the Rusian ruler use "prince" as the translation. While "The Prince" was a sovereign ruler for Machiavelli, by the twentieth century this was, according to the *Oxford English Dictionary*, firmly an "archaic definition" of the word, and it is instead most often used to indicate the son of a ruler, or a subordinate ruler. Thus, though the translation of the title "kniaz'" as "duke" or "prince" may have been accurate enough as early as the fourteenth century and through the twentieth century, the translation is incorrect when read back into earlier periods of medieval history.

Modern Concerns with Translation

In modern English-language work on medieval Rus', "prince" is still the most common translation for kniaz'. Jonathan Shepard and Simon Franklin, two eminent early Slavists, use "prince" in their textbook—*Emergence of Rus*. Janet Martin, whose *Medieval Russia* is assigned in many class-rooms, uses it as well. It is even used in specialist works by the likes of Martin Dimnik, Oleksiy Tolochko, and Nancy Kollman. This book attempts an ambitious change of usage that would affect scholars writing on Rus' itself, particu-larly those focusing on the eleventh and twelfth centuries, as well as those who reference it in their works. In the latter group, an important subset are modern translations of medieval sources, which often mention Rus'; thus, their editors and translators need to deal with Rusian titula-ture. Erling Monsen's edition of the Scandinavian medieval source *Heimskringla* includes the title "king" for Volodimer Sviatoslavich, Iaroslav Vsevolodich, and Vsevolod Iaroslav-ich in the text, but he emends that to "duke" in the foot-notes.[10] James Brundage, in his translation of the thir-teenth-century Henry of Livonia, takes an even stronger editorial stance saying, "Like the 'king' of Polozk, the 'king' of Gerzika was a Russian prince," or earlier, "Vladimir was a Russian prince, not a king, as Henry calls him" (see bk. 1 n. 39; bk. 3 n. 8). Monsen (subtly) and Brundage (aggressively) alter their source texts to change the rank of the Rusian ruler. In his translation of the eleventh-century Thietmar of Merseburg, David Warner is required to deal with Volodimer, the Christianizer of Rus', and though the text refers to him only as "king" (bk. 7, chaps. 72–74), Warner, in his introduction to the text, leads with "king," but then uses "prince" three times to refer to Volodimer (p. 20). These translations of major medieval works by accomplished scholars all change the titulature of the Rusian rulers who play a role in their respective sources. The intent in each of these otherwise excellent editions was, most likely, simply to utilize what they viewed as the accurate title instead of an inaccurate medieval title their source provided. Though they followed the translation accepted by most scholars of Rus', deliberately changing the title of the Rusian ruler in their sources (from "rex" or "konungr") and substituting it for a lower title, is an editorial correction that creates an impression in the mind of the reader, whether student or scholar. It is made clear that the source text is incorrect and that in fact Rusian rulers were not "kings."[11] Thus, they were not the equals of the rulers of England, France, Hungary, or any other "kingdom" in Europe. And while all scholars have dealt with errors in sources, "correcting" titulature that is consistent across sources is highly problematic for creating an accurate perception of the medieval world.

Changing the translation of kniaz' for this period, and thus the perception of the ruler of Rus', is clearly difficult, as can be seen in these few examples. The majority of contemporary scholarship, and English-language scholarship dating back hundreds of years, refers to kniazia as "dukes" or "princes."[12] That, however, should not be taken as evidence of accuracy or appropriateness, but of inertia and, in modern scholarship, of proper citation to other work, which only serves to reinforce the inaccurate translations—what Marshall Poe has referred to as a "cycle of reference."[13] This chapter demonstrates, however briefly, the breadth of the problem inherent in attempting to change this one translation, as well as foreshadowing the echoes that it may have through the scholarship. It may also serve as a challenge to scholars to think more critically about their translation and usage of titulature for medieval officials, whether in their own territory or in others', before proceeding with the previously accepted usage.

Notes

[8] Giles Fletcher, "Of the Russe Commonwealth," in *Rude and Barbarous Kingdom: Russia in the Accounts of Sixteenth-Century English Voyagers*, ed. Lloyd E. Berry and Robert O. Crummey (Madison; University of Wisconsin Press, 1968), p. 145. Other travellers use "duke" as well, such as Sir Thomas Randolph, who met with "the long duke," kniaz' Vyazemskii. Sir Thomas Randolph, "The Account of Sir Thomas Randolph," in *Rude and Barbarous Kingdom*, p. 69. Richard Chancellor translates kniaz' as "duke" in his title of Ivan IV, "The Great Duke of Muscovy and Chief Emperor of Russia," in "The Voyage of Richard Chancellor," in *Rude and Barbarous Kingdom*, p. 26.

[9] For example, the Oxford English Dictionary definition for "Grand Duke" discusses this very thing. "1. a. The title of the sovereigns of certain European countries (called Grand Duchies); the rank so designated is understood to be one degree below that of king. b. In pre-revolutionary Russia, the title of any of the sons of an emperor. (Cf. DUKE 2, 2c.) The title seems to have been first assumed by the ruler of Tuscany in the 16th c. Before Peter the Great, the sovereign of Russia was styled 'Grand Duke of Muscovy' in European diplomacy."

[10] Snorre Sturlason, *Heimskringla or The Lives of the Norse Kings*, ed. Erling Monsen, trans. A. H. Smith (New York: Dover, 1990), p. 118 n. 2.

[11] There is an outlying case to note here, however, which is that of the thirteenth-century rulers of Halych-Volhynia who were granted the title "rex" from the pope, and are often called "king" in English scholarship, especially that written by Ukrainian historians. Andrusiak and Mykytiak, "Kings of Kiev and Galicia"; Isaievych, "On the Titulature of Rulers in Eastern Europe."

[12] It is worth noting, if briefly, that the change advocated here is primarily in regard to English-language scholarship. Though making a kniaz' a king in Ukrainian or Russian (for example) would be a worthy endeavour and historically accurate, the shift would not necessarily be in translation of titulature but in conception of what kniaz' means in this period.

[13] Poe, "*A People Born to Slavery*," pp. 169, 195.

Chapter 3

Titulature and Medieval Rulers

Titulature has actually long been a problem with translating (both literally and metaphorically) the Middle Ages
for the modern world. The meanings and uses of titles
change over time, titles are appropriated from others, and
our modern understanding of titles is actually rather limited. Living in a twenty-first century world where kings,
queens, and nobility are quite rare in one's daily life has
generated a lack of understanding of the nuances of titulature and instead created set notions of the meaning of
words like "king" as a monarch, a sole ruler over a territorial
realm. Attempting to unpack such a concept often leads
to a world of false parallels and equivalencies that affect
both our analysis and our understanding of the medieval
world. However, I would argue that such investigations
are important. We need to delineate specific terms and
concepts to better understand the medieval world on its
own terms. To contextualize the difficulties of working on
Rusian titulature and its complexities, examples will be
shown from various areas of medieval Europe to highlight
the issues inherent in translating medieval rulership.

Late Antiquity

Patrick Geary has written about the issue of historical perception in regard to how Romans viewed those on their

borders. The Romans seem to have been realistic in their appraisal and titulature of their neighbours, especially their enemies, but still attempted to understand the "barbarians" on Roman terms and fit them into a Roman Weltanschauung or world view.[14] (This could be contrasted with the Byzantines who often retained self-consciously archaic terminology for their neighbours, which may have affected their perceptions.) For instance, when the Alamannic confederation attacked in the mid-fourth century they were "led by an uncle and nephew termed 'the most outstanding in power before the other kings,' five kings of second rank, ten *regales*, and a series of magnates."[15] Here we have a nice enumeration of the leadership pyramid of a "barbarian" confederation that also serves quite well to express the problem of translating titulature. There is, in fact, no monarch, but a dual leadership structure, and these two are also implicitly termed kings. Below them are five more kings, but as Geary notes, they are of the second rank, though they bear the same title; they are followed by regales, who are followed by magnates. The situation is still opaque to one not versed in the nuances of the confederation, as there are now roughly seventeen people with the rough title of "ruler," seven of them bearing the title "rex," and ten that of "regales" (lesser kings presumably). Were you to attempt a colloquial English translation of these positions, where would you start? Are the uncle and nephew above all others to be termed "emperors" or "co-emperors" as they rule over "kings"? That might solve the problem in a modern mind, but does it accurately express the contemporary situation? The answer lies instead, as it does throughout, in modifying our modern definition of kingship to avoid the automatic interpretation of "king" as "monarch of a realm," and develop a more complex and nuanced definition to fit the particular medieval, or earlier, situation.

Scandinavia

Moving more properly into the medieval period, it is in the northern world where we see a host of these examples of problematic uses/translations of titulature. (Perhaps there is a connection here to the lack of *Romanitas* present in those places, but this is an issue best left for another discussion so as not to distract from the focus here on titulature.) Eric Christiansen has shown that around the year 800 there were at least forty-five people in Scandinavia bearing the Old Norse title *konungr* (p. 161). This title, which again has the base meaning of ruler, has a problematic translation history into English. In part this is because, just as in the Roman example above, there are konungar (plural of konungr) who report to other konungar. These can be found most easily in the *Heimskringla*, one of the main sources for medieval Scandinavian history, in the section dealing with Harald Fairhair (d. ca. 932), as he is the consolidator of much of Norway under one ruler: himself. In that saga, there are several mentions of multiple konungar, in what appear to be complex political relationships with one another, of varying sorts.[16] Though the *Heimskringla* is a later source, it is often accepted as a relatively accurate portrayal of many items of medieval Scandinavian political structure, and titulature seems to be accurately conveyed there. However, when those titles are translated into modern English, konungr becomes both "chief" and "king" depending upon the interpretation of the modern writer of the medieval konungr's position in the Scandinavian world vis-à-vis other konungar. Anders Winroth seems to play with titulature in his book. He uses "chieftain" regularly to describe rulers known as "konungr" in the primary sources, but he also uses "king" for the Danish rulers, Godfrid, Gorm, and Harald Bluetooth particularly. For Volodimer, whose heirs are known as konungar, he uses "Grand Prince" (pp. 1, 2, 60, 99, 100, 101, 138–41, 143, 145). This is certainly one way to deal with the problem of multiple rulers of varying ranks carrying the same medieval title in the primary sources. The major problem with it is accurately expressed by the authors of *Viking Empires*: "We know the names of some early Scandinavian rulers, but how they were related to each other and how they interacted in Scandinavia we cannot say" (p. 45). Thus, to correctly make the distinctions that Winroth and others make requires a complete understanding of the various power relationships. Even with a complete understanding, such changes still manage to lower the status of one ruler in comparison with another, when both held the same title; the rank and prestige rested with the ruler, not necessarily with the title.

Ireland

Putting to shame the Scandinavians' forty-five konungar, the Irish could boast "no less than 150 kings in the country at any given date between the fifth and twelfth centuries."[17] In Gaelic, these kings were known as *rí*, a word that is cognate with the Latin rex, among other languages' words for ruler.[18] Each rí ruled over his own people, a *túath*, and was responsible for them, and to them. The Irish law codes and codes on status delineate at least three types of rulers, though they fail to identify what is commonly known as a high-king, an *ard-rí*, leading to a great deal of debate in modern scholarship over what the role of such a ruler might have been.[19] The consensus seems to be that there was not a monarchy and that the ard-rí was always, at base, the leader of a túath, and ruled the other *ríthe* (plural of rí) in Ireland because of his personal power, rather than any legal right. (This may be instructive for the Rusian case, where much work has been done trying to find a system, rather than focusing on informal systems of power in regard to the ruler of Kiev's control over the other kniazia.) Even leaving aside the issue of a high-king, there are clearly ranks of rulers in the Irish legal system, there are over-kings and under-kings, and the status codes clearly spell out the ways in which those rulers related to one another. But despite the clear variations in responsibility and title given in the Gaelic, in Latin these rulers are traditionally rendered as "rex," regardless of status as over- or under-king.[20] This tradition of titulature began to change due to political constraints later in the seventeenth century when there was an attempt to create an idea of Irish monarchy read back into the past and the lower level ríthe were termed "chieftains" rather than "kings" (Byrne, p. 41). This modern attempt to revise the titulature exemplifies the problem that is being discussed here. As the meaning of king changed in a world of monarchy and empire, medieval titles and titulature were changed to fit into that model. The Irish case, much like the Scandinavian, is an instructive model for the example of Rus', in that the specifics of context must be examined to best translate the title, and functions, of the ruler. The end result may lead to a more complex rendering than all rulers being called either "king" or "chieftain," but such a problematic situation may also more accurately depict the status of the time.

Anglo-Saxon England

Anglo-Saxon England, already referenced in regard to the claim of the title of *basileus* by various rulers, is another place where a plethora of kings existed. Not only were there a variety of what are traditionally termed kingdoms (Wessex, East Anglia, Mercia, etc.), but within those polities there were other relationships and other people, some of whom bore the same title as the ruler of that land, "king." (This discussion leaves aside the title and position of "Bretwalda." Though it has a similar historiography to the Irish ard-rí, its use for our titulature discussion is minimal, not to mention Patrick Geary's rather unequivocal description of it as "essentially a modern myth.")[21] Asser, in his *Life of King Alfred*, talks primarily about Alfred (d. 899) as a "rex," but he is certainly not the only one who bears that title in his piece. Asser refers to Alfred's relations with the rulers of Mercia and elsewhere as between "reges" (plural of rex), but he also discusses reges who are subordinate to Alfred.[22] One example of this, and also of familial relationships, is when Aethelwulf granted rule to two of his sons when he went to Rome, creating a situation in which all three of them bore the title "rex." This is not an uncommon situation in the medieval world, as has been demonstrated, and Anglo-Saxon England provides just one more example. (I would suggest here, too, that the issue of titulature and its translation is more complex than the dominant diachronic progression towards centralization narrative would suggest.) This complex situation is even acknowledged in one of the Icelandic sagas, potentially authored by Snorri Sturlason (the author of the *Heimskringla* cited above), where it says that Alfred the Great reduced all the tributary kings to the rank of earl, and that under Athelstan (d. 939) there was a rebellion to restore "those who had been kings or princes before."[23] Whether or not a thirteenth-century Icelandic saga is a proper source for tenth-century Anglo-Saxon titulature is a topic that can be debated, but it is certainly an interesting piece of information that does correspond with what Asser's *Life* records regarding the titles of Alfred and his fellow reges. For the purposes of this examination of titulature, the most interesting element is the acknowledgement by another medieval source that a certain historical relationship had existed in which there had been several kings, some tributary to others, and that that relationship changed at a certain point in the late ninth and then the tenth century. Such a commentary on a neighbouring polity's historical power structure and its changes, from only a few hundred years remove, is a valuable addition to this attempt, from the perspective of a thousand years and a multitude of other changes later, to assess the meanings of such titles.

Poland

Moving around Europe to the east, the situation of titulature in medieval Poland is complicated, but in a more traditional fashion. The majority of the discussion of the titulature of medieval Poland has to do with the variability between the Latin titles "dux" and "rex," which were the titles used in both the medieval Polish sources, as well as the German, Bohemian, and papal sources that provide the majority of the information about medieval Poland. The typical differentiation between the two titles is one of independence (rex) versus subordination (dux). Just examining Cosmas of Prague, for example, we can see that dux is the normative title for the majority of Polish rulers, such as Mieszko, Casimir, Władysław, and Bolesław II. It is only Bolesław "Chrobry" who received the title "rex," and that was at the notice of his death.[24] However, even when the title of "rex" was first granted to Bolesław the Brave (d. 1025) circa 1000 it was as part of an attempt by Otto III of the German Empire (d. 1002) to buttress his own imperial title, by having subordinate reges (Althoff, pp. 98–103). The reoccurrence of the title "rex" is debated, but it came most likely at the hands of Pope Gregory VII who crowned Bolesław II (d. ca. 1081), via his legates in 1076, as part of the Investiture Controversy (and an attempt to claim responsibility for reclaiming the Rusian throne for the exiled Iziaslav Iaroslavich (d. 1078) of Rus' who had appealed to him). It is important to note here that I am not suggesting that the title "rex" derives solely from papal endorsement or ecclesiastical coronation. Rulers titled themselves rex without ecclesiastical coronation, or prior to ecclesiastical coronation, in this period. For the chroniclers employed within the German Empire, the issue was more one of subordination to the German ruler, or lack thereof, in determining "rex" or "dux" for the Piast ruler of Poland. Though Bolesław II's coronation has been disputed by German historians, it seems a viable supposition, and the usage of "rex" and "dux" seems to fit the relationship of Poland to the German Empire as viewed from the traditional medieval perspective (Cowdrey, p. 452). The picture changes slightly, however, when we add in other sources that discuss the Polish rulers and their titulature. The Scandinavian *Heimskringla* refers to Bolesław as a "konungr" in several places,[25] while the Rusian chronicles give the Polish rulers the title "kniaz'."[26] Both of these sources have as much validity as the German, Bohemian, and Polish sources in describing their neighbour, marital partner, ally, and enemy. The konungr of the *Heimskringla* fits the Polish ruler, unsurprisingly, into a world in which that title may be used for a variety of rulers, of differing levels of superiority; thus, potentially, fitting both the "dux" and "rex" conceptions that the Latin conveys. The Old East Slavic kniaz' is a traditional title for Slavic rulers, and was the title used by the Rusian chroniclers for their own rulers as well. However, these Scandinavian and Rusian titles play little role in the modern translation of the titles of the Polish rulers who are rendered as "dukes" or "kings" exclusively depending upon the Latin titles. This is a perfectly acceptable rendering, but one that does not fully utilize the breadth of sources available to the modern scholar, nor one that acknowledges the complexities inherent in these discussions of titulature, especially in this region.

The point of such a brief tour of medieval titulature should be clear: the world of medieval titles is more complicated than it appears at first blush, or in most works of modern scholarship. For every clear-cut delineation of a hierarchical power structure, there are a dozen examples of conflicting titles. "Rex" is translated into English as "king" in almost every case, but "konungr" is only sometimes translated into English as "king," depending upon the scholar, and that person's perception of the politics of the particular situation. "Rí" and "ard-rí" fulfill similar roles in an ever-changing and sometimes ambiguous hierarchical structure. The situation just briefly discussed already cries out for a wholesale reexamination of titulature, including an extended discussion of modern bias in regard to who gets which title and when. Further, it appears that the titles most often changed in translation appear on the periphery of the "traditional" medieval Europe discussed in chapter 1. For our purposes here, the examples in this chapter suggest that the more data historians can collect regarding titulature, the more care they can take to create accurate understanding in the mind of their readers through thoughtful titulature choices, which will then benefit not just Rus', but our understanding of Europe and European interactions as a whole.

Notes

[14] Patrick J. Geary, "Barbarians and Ethnicity," in *Late Antiquity: A Guide to the Postclassical World*, ed. Peter Brown, G. W. Bowersock, and Oleg Grabar (Cambridge, MA: Harvard University Press, 1999).

[15] Geary, "Barbarians and Ethnicity," p. 112.

[16] Snorri Sturluson, *Heimskringla*, ed. Bjarni Adalbjarnarson, vol. 1 (Reykjavík: Hid Íslenzka Fornritagélag, 1951), pp. 94, 99, 103–04.

[17] Francis John Byrne, *Irish Kings and High-Kings* (Dublin: Four Courts, 1973; 2nd ed., 2001), p. 7. Bart Jaski scaled that number back to just 100, but noted that it was a constantly changing figure; either way, it is rather large. Bart Jaski, *Early Irish Kingship and Succession* (Dublin: Four Courts, 2000), p. 37

[18] Byrne, *Irish Kings and High-Kings*, p. 41; Jaski, *Early Irish Kingship*, p. 38.

[19] It is worth noting here that there has been an immense amount written about the issue of kingship in Ireland and that this discussion simplifies much of that to provide a mere glimpse at the issue as part of a comparative survey. For just a bare few examples on this topic see Charles Doherty, "Kingship in Early Ireland," in *The Kingship and Landscape of Tara*, ed. Edel Bhreathnach (Dublin: Four Courts, 2005), pp. 12–13; Byrne, *Irish Kings and High-Kings*, pp. 42–43, 256–71; T. M. Charles-Edwards, *Early Christian Ireland* (Cambridge: Cambridge University Press, 2000), pp. 482, 519–20.

[20] Byrne, *Irish Kings and High-Kings*, pp. 7, 259. There are some variations, however, as St. Patrick in his letter used both "reges" and "regules" to refer to Irish rulers in different letters, though without any seeming consistency. Doherty, "Kingship in Early Ireland," pp. 3–4.

[21] Geary, "Barbarians and Ethnicity," p. 127.

[22] Asser, "Life of King Alfred," trans. Simon Keynes and Michael Lapidge, in *Alfred the Great: Asser's* Life of King Alfred *and other Contemporary Sources* (New York: Penguin, 1983), chap. 80; Asser, *Annales Rerum Gestarum Alfredi Magni*, trans. Franciscus Wise (1722), p. 49. For Aethelwulf, "Life of King Alfred," chap. 12.

[23] "Egil's Saga," trans. Bernard Scudder, in *The Sagas of the Icelanders: A Selection* (New York: Viking, 2001), p. 81.

[24] "Cosmae chronica Boemorum," ed. D. Rudolfo Köpke, *Monumenta Germaniae Historica Scriptores 9*, ed. George Pertz (Hannover, 1851), bk. 2, chaps. 2, 5, 20; bk. 3, chaps. 16, 27, 34, 35, 36, 41, 51. For Bolesław I as rex, see bk. 1, chap. 41, though the translator of the English edition of *Cosmas* also notes that he does not record Bolesław's elevation to that title. *The Chronicle of the Czechs by*

Cosmas of Prague, trans. Lisa Wolverton (Washington, DC: Catholic University of America Press, 2009), n. 339. Gallus Anonymous provides a (more) native check on that titulature, *Gesta Principum Polonorum: The Deeds of the Princes of the Poles*, ed. and trans. Paul W. Knoll and Frank Schaer (New York: Central European University Press, 2003), p. 37 (for the crowning by Otto III), and n. 116 (for other possible coronations of Polish rulers).

[25] *Heimskringla*, 1:253, 341, 342, 343.

[26] The *Povest' vremennykh let* (PVL) refers to the Polish ruler as "kniaz'" (pp. 996, 1102), as does the Kievan Chronicle (p. 1146, among other places) and the Bohemian ruler the same way (p. 1149). Donald Ostrowski's paradosis has been used for this work, though citations are by year so that one may use the English, or a Russian version, as needed. *The Povest' vremennykh let: An Interlinear Collation and Paradosis*, ed. Donald Ostrowski, David Birnbaum, and Horace G. Lunt (Cambridge, MA: Harvard University Press, 2004), online at http://clover.slavic.pitt.edu/pvl/ost1.html; PVL, s.a. 1102, *Ipat'evskaia letopis'*, vol. 2, Polnoe sobranie russkikh letopisei (Moscow: Iazyki slavianskoi kul'tury, 2001) (hereafter Hypatian Chronicle), s.a. 1146, 1149.

Chapter 4

What Was a Kniaz'?

The title left unexamined in the preceding chapter is the
one to which the bulk of this book is devoted and that is
the Slavic title "kniaz'" (князь). The basic functions of the
kniazia in Rus' (ruler, military leader, lawgiver, and tax collector) were the same as for most rulers throughout medieval Europe, and the varying power relationships were
similar to what has already been shown in the examples
of the last chapter. At different times in the eleventh and
twelfth centuries there were kniazia subordinate to others
bearing the same title, power relations between them
being dependent upon personal power rather than titulature. Though this is complicated in our modern world, it
seems to have been understandable, and broadly used,
in the medieval world. Before embarking upon an examination of the usage of the title "kniaz'," as well as the foreign titles for Rusian rulers (in chapter 5), it might be useful to have an understanding of the word itself, as well as
an appreciation for what some of the functions of a kniaz'
were, based upon the primary sources, so that the most
accurate construction of a title, and translation of both
sense and meaning, can be achieved.

The word "kniaz'" comes from the Germanic root *kuningaz, the same root for such words as the German "Koenig,"
the Anglo-Saxon "cyning," Scandinavian "konungr," and of

course the modern English "king."[27] The root meaning of this word is simply "ruler," or perhaps "chief," and as the group of people (originally a clan or family) grew larger in size and their political organization grew in complexity, the responsibilities of the ruler may have changed over time as well. But the basic titulature stayed the same, from the same root, and at a simplistic level all of these titles break down simply to "ruler."

The functions of a ruler grant us a view into the increasing specialization of the political process, but also allow for a classification of who the ruler was, and what an accurate title for that ruler might be. This section is by no means intended as an exhaustive examination of the role of the ruler in Rus'. The most recent, in-depth, work on that subject is in Russian, and was written just after the fall of the Soviet Union by A. P. Tolochko. In it, he addresses the role of the kniaz' in Rus', and how it changed over the course of the dissolution of the Kievan period. Although it is a thorough work of scholarship, it is inaccessible to the majority of medieval historians, not to mention general readers, who do not work in Russian.[28] This section is not intended to duplicate that work. Rather than provide an exhaustive catalogue of duties, this section simply highlights some examples of the role of the kniaz' as a window into titulature.

Who Was a Kniaz'

An important place to begin an overview of the Rusian kniazia is an acknowledgement that there were several of them at any one time, but that the title did have a specific value. In Rus' of the eleventh and twelfth centuries the title "kniaz'" only appeared for a ruler of a territory, typically based in a city (Kiev, Novgorod, Volodimer, Polotsk, Chernigov, and so on), with a surrounding region under his control as well. Never do the sources give someone the title "kniaz'" who did not have or control territory. The title then clearly indicates a claim to rule over something, rather than simply inheritance or birthright. (The title "kniaz'" would, over time, shift to accommodate this meaning, as will be discussed briefly later in this book.) In contrast, in the variety of kingdoms that use the title "prince," the current typical translation of kniaz', the title is bestowed at birth on the male child of a king. It is part of the boy's, and later man's, life, despite whatever other positions he may hold. (A contemporary example would be Prince William of England who was titled as such when he was born, though he holds, and has held, other titles in his life, such as duke of Cambridge.) Thus, its importance is as a symbol of his descent from the ruler of the kingdom, rather than any particular power over territory, or a specific position. As can be seen, this stark contrast helps elucidate the problems inherent in the current translation of kniaz' as "prince."

This situation of kniazia ruling over other kniazia may have begun in Rus' with the creation of a hierarchy of rulership in which the ruler of Kiev assigned subordinate cities and towns to his children for them to rule as his proxies. The *Povest' vremenennykh let* (PVL), our earliest and almost only source for early Rus', records that it was Sviatoslav (d. 972) who did this first, before heading off to attempt to conquer Bulgaria on the Danube. But it is most associated with Volodimer, who assigned his many children to cities in 988, and with his son Iaroslav the Wise both prior to and at his death in 1054 (PVL, s.a. 988, 1054). It is also at this time that we see a reinforcement of the hierarchy of the rulers of Rus', as Iaroslav tells his sons to honour Iziaslav (their eldest surviving brother whom Iaroslav placed in Kiev), as they have honoured Iaroslav himself (PVL, s.a. 1054). Despite the assignment of territories by Volodimer and Iaroslav, and despite the use of the same titles for all involved, it was clear that the ruler of Kiev was the *pater familias* (either actually or metaphorically) of the entire Volodimerovichi clan, at least until the second quarter of the twelfth century. Many examples could be given of the ruler of Kiev as the pater familias. The death of Iaroslav and the installation of new rulers has been noted, but when new rulers assumed the throne of Kiev, they often assigned territories to their family members as part of that installation, such as when Vsevolod inherited Kiev in 1078. Similarly, upon Vsevolod's death, there is an encomium to him in which it is stated that his relatives demanded territories from him, and that he bestowed territories upon them; thus reinforcing the idea of the ruler of Kiev as the appointer of rulers to territories. Finally, the PVL notes that in 1036 after the death of Iaroslav's brother Mstislav, Iaroslav was now the "sole ruler in Rus'," despite the presence of others bearing the title "kniaz'" (PVL, s.a. 1078, 1093, 1036).

One title for such a ruler has been *velikii kniaz'*, often translated as "Grand Prince." This title parallels the Irish ard-rí noted earlier, and has been used as such in examinations of Rus'. Though there is some disagreement in the scholarship, the majority position is that in this period, the title is used neither particularly frequently by chroniclers nor with any political consistency. Some have suggested that it means the eldest member of the kindred, while others suggest it is a panegyric to a deceased ruler, similar to the use of "tsar'" discussed below.[29] Though it might be nice to use it to indicate an over-king of Rus', that does not seem to have been the contemporary usage, and so the focus of the study must remain on the basic title, and translation, of kniaz' itself.

Kniaz' at War

One of the traditional features of a ruler, in most any territory and period, is the ability to call troops to war, and this
is certainly true of the kniazia of Rus' as well. All of them
were able to call upon not only their own warband (*dru-
zhina*), but local troops as well (admittedly less frequently),
and the ruler of Kiev was able to call troops from throughout the regions of Rus', via their respective kniazia, to
go to war together against common foes. (One must, of
course, acknowledge that this is an ideal case scenario.
Cases may be found where townspeople refused to support their kniaz', where kniazia rose in rebellion against the
kniaz' of Kiev, and so on.) This is quite similar to the brief
picture that Peter Sawyer paints of Scandinavian kings who
made war with their warbands, but were also able to call
upon larger communities of "allies and tributary warriors"
and even townsmen for the purposes of defence (Sawyer,
pp. 91–92). Particularly after the death of Iaroslav the Wise,
this becomes evident for the kniazia when his son Iziaslav
in Kiev, acting with his brothers Sviatoslav (d. 1077) and
Vsevolod, summoned troops for the defence of Rus'—in
1060 against the Torks, and in 1067 against Vseslav Bri-
acheslavich of Polotsk (d. 1101) after he took Novgorod
(PVL, s.a. 1060 and 1067). This is one of the main features
of the ruler of Kiev, as paterfamilias, that they are able to
summon troops, typically via their respective kniazia, from
throughout Rus' to go to war against a common enemy.
The same is seen even when Vsevolod Olgovich (d. 1146),
a usurper in the sense that he was ineligible according to
the common understanding of the rules of succession to
the throne of Kiev, was still able to summon soldiers from
throughout Rus', including Novgorod, which had often gone
its own way.[30] (The common understanding of the succession politics is that if one's father did not sit on a particu-

lar throne, Kiev is the most common example, then that person was ineligible to rule there.) But even on a more local level, this same phenomenon can be seen as rulers summoned soldiers from their regions and towns to go to war, often with one another. In 1096, the PVL records a conflict in which Oleg Sviatoslavich (d. 1115) made war upon Iziaslav Volodimerich (d. 1096), who had usurped territory belonging to Oleg. To create his army, Oleg gathered men from Smolensk, while Iziaslav assembled troops from Suzdal', Rostov, and Beloozero. Other parties, later in the entry, convened for a campaign against Oleg as well, and similarly gathered men from their tributary territories. This becomes a commonplace in the growing internecine conflict at the end of the eleventh and beginning of the twelfth centuries, as the Volodimerovichi battled one another for precedence and land. In each case, a ruler with the title "kniaz'," connected to a territory that he ruled, was able to summon troops from that territory.

Kniaz' as Lawgiver

Another of the traditional functions of a medieval ruler is as lawgiver, and this one exists in Rus' as well, and serves as a way to point out both the similarities and di
between Rusian rulers and those in the rest of Europe. The initial law code in Rus' is entitled the *Russkaia Pravda* and was codified by Iaroslav the Wise.[31] This is exceedingly similar to what is seen elsewhere in Europe: for instance, Stephen of Hungary (d. 1038) (or his eventual successor Andrew), at about the same time as Iaroslav, codified a series of decrees and laws into the first law code of Hungary (Berend, Urbańczyk, and Wiszewski, p. 158). Iaroslav as "sole ruler" of Rus' was well within his rights to establish a law code, or more accurately to codify some existing legal practices, but his sons di

norm. The next iteration of the Russkaia Pravda is known as the Pravda of Iaroslav's sons (Iziaslav, Sviatoslav, and Vsevolod), who jointly agreed on a law code and promulgated it throughout Rus', much as they had summoned troops jointly to war on their enemies.[32] Pointing out both the similarities and differences in regard to wider issues of European conceptions of rulership, the next generation met at Liubech in 1097 to conclude a peace treaty and a new understanding of Rusian territorial divisions (PVL, s.a. 1097). Six different kniazia representing the major branches of the ruling Volodimerovichi family of Rus' met and responded to the recent spate of internecine conflicts, with an attempt to codify their understanding of territory and responsibility, as a corporate understanding of the kniazia. (This requires one to keep in mind that all kniazia were members of the Volodimerovichi clan, and thus kin.)[33] In this sense, the rulers met to collectively adjudicate conflict within the larger Volodimerovichi clan and rule corporately, at least to some extent. They were not, however, making law corporately anymore. In fact, their meeting points out the increasing differences between them in their administration of their own territories and their own families, which are growing ever more separate as the clan grows in number. In this way, the Volodimerovichi are unlike the traditional image of a western European ruler, as they are not often judges, relying more on common law and *wergild* (man price) practices that tend to keep the peace, but not to directly involve them. But they are still quite similar to other rulers, such as the Irish, whose multiplicity of kings often entered into contractual arrangements with one another as a way to more effectively share power and govern collectively (Byrne, pp. 43–45). This calls into question the dominance of the traditional model of what a ruler was, once again, and suggests a further reexamination of the constituent elements of kingship in medieval Europe.

Kniaz' as Tax Collector

Another function of these kniazia that is shared amongst rulers is that of tax collector, or tribute taker. In early Rus', taking tribute irregularly was what got one of the early rulers, Igor (d. 945), killed by the Derevlians, reinforcing not just the story of his wife's vengeance, but also the importance of regular tribute collection (and no more) (PVL, s.a. 945). Later Russian rulers also took tribute from the regions they ruled, and took care to define those territories and protect them from others, especially other kniazia. However, it should be noted that there is some evidence for a remittance of taxation to the ruler of Kiev by other kniazia. For instance, the lack of such a remittance in 1014 by Iaroslav (before he was "the Wise") in Novgorod to his father Volodimer in Kiev almost led to war (PVL, s.a. 1014). This suggests, though evidence in this period is sparse, another means of categorizing the hierarchy of kniazia in Rus'. The division of taxation or tribute-taking regions mirrored the territorial divisions of the various kniazia. A kniaz' was allowed to take tribute/taxes within the city and surrounding territory that he ruled. When those boundaries were crossed, and they often were, protests were made to someone (often the kniaz' in Kiev) and/or conflict ensued.[34] The kniazia of Rus' also assembled collectively to divide up the tribute-taking areas to minimize such conflicts as they did in 1146, with an extended discussion of tribute taking in the northeastern territories along the River Volga (Hypatian Chronicle, s.a. 1146). Simon Franklin notes the importance of these activities in regard to the construction of Russian kingdoms by saying, "the organization and policing of trade- and tribute-routes contributed to the consolidation and growth of a polity under princely rule" (Franklin and Shepard, p. 334). Though the language used is often different, similar policies can be seen in regard to polities elsewhere in Europe. In Scandinavia (Sawyer, p. 91) and in the Ottonian and Salian lands (Bernhardt, p. 38), tribute was taken from subordinate peoples. However, in the secondary sources, scholars often talk about taxes in a different way than our meagre sources for Rus' would allow.[35] This may give the impression of difference in implementation when it is rather, more likely, a difference in source base. Similarly, there are other taxes/tributes due to a ruler, such as the requirement to host an itinerant ruler on his travels throughout his realm. This is discussed in some depth for Ottonian and Salian rulers of the German Empire (Bernhardt, pp. 56–60), but is also known elsewhere in Europe (Sawyer, p. 91). Unfortunately, though we can say that the Rusian kniazia were itinerant to a degree, as John Bernhardt also notes (p. 47), there are no extant sources that preserve the requirement to host these rulers on their perambulations. Though there are difficulties with the Rusian source base, the information we do have shows the Rusian kniazia taking part in another of the key aspects of being a premodern ruler, that of the right of tribute taking/taxation in their realm.

This chapter not only covers the basic functions of the kniaz', but highlights the clear similarities elsewhere in Europe, specifically the Germanic territories, but also Poland, Hungary, and Ireland. The examples shown here demonstrate times when the ruler of Kiev may act independently, and other times when the rulers of the territories of Rus' act corporately. Such action may depend on the type of threat or the period in Rusian history, but there is little, if any, way to create a clear separation using translation between the kniaz' of Kiev and the kniazia of the other territories that is workable throughout the eleventh and twelfth centuries entirely. Each of those kniazia held some, if not all, functions of a ruler, especially acting as military leader and tax collector, and often a lawgiver.

Their exercise of those functions both singularly and collectively makes it difficult, if not impossible, to differentiate between them using titulature at this time, adding another layer to our understanding of the construction of medieval titles and their uses by medieval peoples.

Notes

[27] Maks Fasmer, *Etimologicheskii slovar' russkogo iazyka*, vol. 2 (Moscow: Progress, 1986), p. 266. With thanks to Bill Darden at the University of Chicago for assisting me with understanding the linguistics background to this. See also Andrusiak and Mykytiak, "Kings of Kiev and Galicia," p. 342. Iaroslav Isaievych notes a slightly different derivation, though only in passing. Iaroslav Isaievych, "On the Titulature of Rulers in Eastern Europe," *Journal of Ukrainian Studies* 29 (2004): 219.

[28] Similarly, Piotr Boroń has written a monograph about the titulature of Slavic rulers, with Rusian rulers included, in the tenth through twelfth centuries. The book, in Polish, does little to elucidate the understanding of a Western medieval audience that does not read Polish scholarship. Even in this thorough and well-grounded discussion of titulature, however, kniaz' is translated in the brief English summary as "prince." Piotr Boroń, *Kniaziowie, królowie, carowie...:Tytuły i nazwy władców słowiańskich we wczesnym średniowieczu* (Katowice: Wydawnictwo Uniwersytetu Śląskiego, 2010). Thank you to Jakub Kabala for bringing this work to my attention, and finding a version for me.

[29] Tolochko, *kniaz' v drevnei Rusi*, pp. 127–35; Andrzej Poppe, "On the Title of the Grand Prince in the Tale of Ihor's Campaign," in *Eucharisterion: Essays Presented to Omeljan Pritsak on His Sixtieth Birthday by his Colleagues and Students*, ed. Ihor Ševčenko and Frank E. Sysn, with the assistance of Uliana M. Pasicznyk, Harvard Ukrainian Studies 3–4 (Cambridge, MA: Ukrainian Research Institute, 1979–80), pp. 684–85. The outlier, though most recent, is Martin Dimnik, who suggests that the title was used regularly by the ruler of Kiev from Iaroslav the Wise forward. Martin Dimnik, "The Title 'Grand Prince' in Kievan Rus'," *Mediaeval Studies* 66 (2004): 253–312. There is substantial scholarship on this matter, that Tolochko has covered briefly, and Poppe more fully in his, "Words that Serve the Authority: On the Title of 'Grand Prince' in Kievan Rus'," in *Christian Russia in the Making* (Aldershot: Ashgate, 2007), pp. 159–91. Tolochko suggests that it means the senior member of the kindred, utilizing non-chronicle sources, while Poppe believes that was a panegyric. Tolochko, *kniaz' v drevnei Rusi*, p. 133; Poppe, "On the Title of the Grand Prince," pp. 684–85.

[30] Hypatian Chronicle, for example, s.a. 1144. Especially after 1136, Novgorod was much more likely to be independent of the will of Kiev, though absolutely participating in the larger world of

Rusian politics, bringing in the most advantageous kniaz' possible to increase its own standing vis-à-vis the larger Rusian world.

[31] This is largely accepted, and is based upon internal attribution within the *Pravda*, even though the copies are extant only from much later. Daniel Kaiser, *The Growth of the Law in Medieval Russia* (Princeton: Princeton University Press, 1980), p. 43. Many of the laws in what is known as "Iaroslav's Pravda" deal with the Varangians and crimes committed by them or against them, leading some to believe that it was created specifically in, or for, Novgorod, where they had a larger presence. Simon Franklin, as well, notes that the role of Christian lawgiver may have motivated Iaroslav (p. 221). Franklin and Shepard, *Emergence of Rus'*, pp. 219–24.

[32] Franklin and Shepard, *Emergence of Rus'*, pp. 286–88; Kaiser, *Growth of the Law*, p. 43. This cooperation may be more a feature of the chroniclers than reality.

[33] Both A. V. Nazarenko and A. P. Tolochko have written about the corporate nature of rule amongst the Volodimerovichi as well. A. V. Nazarenko, "Rodovoi siuzerenitet riurikovichei nad rus'iu (X–XI vv.)," *Drevneishie gosudarstva na territorii SSSR* (1985): 149–57; A. P. Tolocho, *Kniaz' v drevnei Rusi*, p. 132.

[34] An example of which is the complaint of Novgorod that the kniaz' of Rostov was taking tribute in Novgorodian territory. Hypatian Chronicle, s.a. 1148. This entry is discussed in more detail in Franklin and Shepard, *Emergence of Rus'*, p. 334.

[35] George Vernadsky notes this specifically in his discussion of finance in Rus' by saying that a regular taxation system was established, but that the language used for it was the same as for tribute taking, and thus he would continue to use "tribute" to describe it. George Vernadsky. *Kievan Russia*, 2nd ed. (New Haven: Yale University Press, 1976), pp. 189–92, 190, for the specific quotation regarding the use of the word "tribute." A related situation exists in Poland, where the earliest chronicle, that of Gallus Anonymous, does not provide sufficient information for taxation, but there is information about tribute. It is only in the later period, beginning in the thirteenth century, that there is a more standardized system of practice. Berend, Urbańczyk, and Wiszewski, *Central Europe in the High Middle Ages*, pp. 282–83.

Chapter 5

Medieval Titulature and Rus'

Rus' was, in the eleventh and twelfth centuries, part and parcel of the larger medieval European world. Conceptualizing it this way is an asset when attempting to comprehend the nature of a kniaz'. A comparison can then be made of medieval sources from different languages and kingdoms that were roughly contemporary with the period under investigation. This framework will allow us to better understand what a kniaz' was, and what the proper meaning, and translation, of the title should be. In this chapter, sources from around the Latin-writing world, Scandinavia, Byzantium, Rus', and even an example from Middle Low German will be examined to see how contemporaries referred to the rulers of Rus', in an attempt to find the most accurate way of understanding, and replicating, medieval titulature.

Latin Sources (and one Middle Low German Source)

Rus' appears throughout Latin chronicles, in both large and small mentions, and the ruler of Rus' is almost uniformly referred to as "rex." In chronicles from the German Empire, Lambert of Hersefeld under the year 1075 refers to a "Ruzenorum Rex," while the Annales Augustani refer to the daughter of the ruler as, "Rutenorum regis filiam."[36] In a series of more substantial mentions from a directly contemporaneous source, Thietmar of Merseburg refers to the ruler of Rus' consistently as "rex" throughout his text, even while disapproving of Volodimer as a "fornicatur immensus."[37] Annalista Saxo changes what is ruled from people to territory to call the ruler, "regi de Ruzia."[38] One of the rare Latin sources that does not refer to the ruler of Rus' as a "rex" is the work of Bruno of Querfurt; he actually journeyed to Rus' in the early eleventh century, motivated by the proselytizing passion of Otto III. Bruno, who met Volodimer and considered him a good Christian, referred to him simply as "senior Ruzorum."[39] What reason there might be for this difference in title is difficult to judge, but Bruno was ecumenical in his use of the title "senior," using it for Bolesław of Poland, the ruler of the Swedes, as well as Otto III's successor Henry II (d. 1024). Bruno's focus was on Christianization of the pagans, not titulature, and so referring to the rulers he encountered or dealt with as "leader" (or "sovereign" as Soloviev translates it, p. 150) seems to be an acceptable shorthand to let him proceed on his way. It also includes the ruler of Rus', once again, on par with others in the medieval world who might otherwise be known as kings.

The complicated internal political realm of Rus' is acknowledged by Abbot Wilhelm, who was attempting to construct a twelfth-century genealogy for a marital dispute with the French king. In his genealogy, he refers to Rus' repeatedly, as the Rusians were married into both the Danish and French royal lines (see Raffensperger, *Ties of Kinship*). Most tellingly, he says of Rus': "nam plures ibi reges sunt" (for there are many kings/reges there).[40] Wilhelm was correct: as has been shown, there were many reges in Rus', leaving the modern reader with only the question of how to properly deal with, and translate, the idea that Wilhelm was so clear about. Not as clear as Wilhelm's statement, but perhaps more tantalizing, is Siegebert of Gembloux's account of the usurpation of Iziaslav's rule in Kiev by his brother Sviatoslav in the 1070s. Siegebert tells of Iziaslav's expulsion, as well as Iziaslav's flight to the court of Henry IV and his subsequent request for help there. However, Siegebert's most interesting phrase is "alter eorum a consortio regni pulsus."[41] If we take this to mean that there was within Rus' a "fellowship of rule," then the statement becomes similar to that of Wilhelm, acknowledging that there were several rulers within Rus' bearing the same title of "rex." Such a situation, as we have seen, would not be unusual, but this additional evidence helps us contextualize the contemporary understanding of events; it also suggests that these commentators knew the situation within Rus' and were not simply applying a more familiar terminology to an unfamiliar place.[42]

Henry of Livonia, writing in the next century, details the numerous interactions between the rulers of various Rusian cities and regions with the crusaders in Livonia. Though Henry has little liking for the Rusians, his main characters interact with Rus' a great deal and these rulers, always bearing the title "rex," pop up repeatedly in his text, whether they are ruling Pskov, Novgorod, or a variety of other Rusian cities.[43] Pope Innocent IV (d. 1254) adds another instance of the title of "rex" for the ruler of Novgorod, in this case Alexander "Nevsky" (d. 1263), with a mid-thirteenth century letter. However, in a separate communication to Alexander, the pope addresses him as "dux" of Suzdal, utilizing a different title for a different place in which Alexander rules.[44] As will be seen below for an earlier period, the pope has a variety of titles upon which to draw for medieval rulers. Why then, does he use "rex" in one instance and "dux" in another? The specifics of this interaction between the papacy and Alexander Nevsky involve the Mongols, Baltic crusades, and Alexander's own brother and are outside the scope of this inquiry, but Innocent IV's use of both titles does confirm that the titulature used by popes, and thus perhaps others, is deliberate, and therefore to be valued in any attempt to understand medieval perceptions of rulership.

Continuing to stay slightly far afield chronologically, in the thirteenth century the Hanseatic League began to create a series of trading treaties in the eastern Baltic, which included Rusian cities such as Novgorod and Pskov. Extant copies of these treaties exist in Middle Low German, such as for the 1269 treaty between Lübeck and Novgorod, in which the ruler of Novgorod is referred to multiple times as "*coning*,"[45] a word that shares the same Germanic root of *kuningaz with kniaz' itself. Both of these examples are particularly useful to us, because the writers of these documents knew the milieu, if not the participants themselves, which suggests that, once again, their use of titulature was deliberate and not simply imitative of their own experience.

These Latin texts (and one German text), just a representative sampling of the whole body of sources from across three centuries and several political territories, were written with different purposes, though none of them was intended to glorify Rus' or to necessarily create a particular image of Rusian kingship in the minds of the reader. Their mentions of Rus' and of Rusian rulership are often incidental, and thus more interesting and persuasive to medievalists, especially as they use (again almost uniformly) the same titulature for these rulers.

One must note as well, that this is not because of a lack of language for titulature in medieval Latin. As stated in the previous chapter, Polish rulers are almost always referred to as "dux"; the title "princeps" is used on occasion for rulers beyond the bounds of the first Carolingian, and later German Empire;[46] and the *Historia Norvegiae* even uses "regulus" in the places we might expect to simply find "konungr" in an Old Norse history of the region, such as Heimskringla.[47] Karl Werner expressed the complexity of eleventh-century titulature by looking at the Register of Pope Gregory VII:

> A glance at the *Register* of Gregory VII is enough to show a true picture of eleventh-century conditions. There are 152 lay addressees in Gregory's register, including, besides forty-five kings, eighty princes: the dukes of Poland and Bohemia, the princes of Salerno, Capua and Benevento, *dux* Beatrix, Duke Godfrey and the Margravess Mathilda, the doge of Venice, Duke Robert Guiscard of Apulia, Calabria and Sicily, Margrave Azzo of Este, the dukes of Suabia, Bavaria, Carinthia, Lotharingia and Saxony, the margrave of the Saxon East Mark, the dukes of Normany, Acquitaine and Burgundy, the counts of Flanders, Brittany, Blois-Champagne, Anjou, Toulouse and Provence, to name only the most important.[48]

Within that one-hundred and fifty-two, Rus' appears amongst the kings rather than anywhere else, encapsulating the idea that there were many titles to choose from in Latin, and the one chosen to delineate the Rusian rulers was chosen specifically. This choice should not be underestimated. There was a wealth of titulature to describe medieval rulers of varying statuses in Latin: to give just one example, Bruno of Querfurt used "senior" for Volodimer of Rus', Bolesław of Poland, and Henry II of the German Empire.[49] But the title used by the majority of Latin sources for the rulers of Rus' was not "senior," "dux," or "princeps," but "rex." It seems quite unlikely that this happened due to chance, and much more likely that it reflects a particular understanding (correct or otherwise) of the situation in regard to the rulers of Rus'.

Old Norse Sources

The Old Norse sources discussed in chapter 3 in relation to issues of medieval titulature and the picture there for rulers of Rus' should not be surprising. Whether it is in *Heimskringla*, *Morkinskinna*, or *Fagrskinna* (the three main Old Norse language sources for this period), the ruler of Rus' is referred to as a "konungr."[50] Towards the end of *Heimskringla*, where the author notes a relationship between the rulers of Norway, Rus', and Denmark, all three—Mstislav Volodimerich (noted in the text by the name Harald due to his descent from Harold Godwinsson) (d. 1132), Valdemar of Denmark (d. 1182), and Magnus of Norway (d. 1139)—are each called "konungr" in one sentence.[51] It was seemingly a given for the writers of these sources that the rulers of Rus', originally Scandinavian and connected to the region through multiple marriages, carried the same title as their rulers at home. Interestingly, the name given to Rus' in Old Norse, "Gardariki," does give some sense of the larger issue under discussion about Rus', however, as it indicates a kingdom of cities. This is, in many ways, an accurate description of Rus', both due to the political division of the territory by cities and their surrounding regions, and also because the power centres (as with most medieval kingdoms) lay with the cities, rather than anywhere else.

Byzantine Greek Sources

It is with the Byzantines and their sources that most of the trouble lies, as well as the majority of historiographical problems. The traditional position of Rus' in the medieval world has been seen to be within what was called the Byzantine Commonwealth, and while scholarship is being written that aims to change that, it is a difficult model to break after dominating the historiography for nearly half a century. (See Raffensperger, *Reimagining Europe*, chap. 1, or Kaldellis, *Hellenism in Byzantium*, pp. 109–10.) In many eyes still, the image of Rus' that is maintained in Byzantium must then be the most accurate of all of these sources, due to their close connection. This is untrue, however, and the Byzantine sources for non-Byzantines are often problematic. For instance, the *De Administrando Imperio*, one of the most well-known sources of the tenth century for its image of the lands surrounding Byzantium, was out of date by the time it was written and relied heavily on information that should have been treated more sceptically.[52] Anna Komnena, writing in the twelfth century about the reign of her father from the eleventh through the twelfth centuries, does not refer to Rus' once in that time when Rus' is actively marrying into families throughout Europe; she does mention many other major European kingdoms, their soldiery, and dynastic marriages. Further, as Peter Frankopan notes, "The terms Kelt, Latin, Frank and Norman are used interchangeably, vaguely and inconsistently by Anna Komnene" (Anna Comnena, bk. 1, chap. 1, n. 5).

Within this frame, Rus' and Rusian leaders do appear in Byzantine sources, if rarely, and they are usually given the title "arkhon" or "arkhontissa," as in the case of Ol'ga of Rus' who acted as the regent for Sviatoslav in the tenth century.[53] "Arkhon," another title that originally simply meant ruler, had by the eleventh century come to be used for Slavic rulers in the Peloponnesus, as well as for some rulers around the Black Sea.[54] For instance, there was a *protospatharios* and *strategos* named George Tzoulas stationed in Cherson in the eleventh century who was also called arkhon of the Khazars (well after the dissolution of the Khazar Kaganate), to delineate his power over the Khazars from his imperial positions.[55] This Byzantine titulature for the Rusian rulers, though not the Greek basileus or the Hellenized Latin Ῥήξ (rex) used for some western kings, does depict the Rusian ruler as the leader of his own group, albeit one inferior to the Byzantine emperor, a category in which the ruler of the Rusians most likely found himself in good company.

Rusian Sources

Within Rus', the sources use the title "kniaz'" for rulers from the Volodimerovichi family, as well as for some foreign rulers. And much like the Scandinavian and Anglo-Saxon sources, they seem comfortable with a degree of uncertainty in terms of hierarchy, as some kniazia are referred to as being more senior to other kniazia. One example from 1078 might point this out most clearly. In that year, Oleg Sviatoslavich and Boris Viacheslavich (d. 1078), two members of the Volodimerovichi clan, were engaged in a conflict with other members of the clan. The army that marched out to meet them was led by four other members of the clan (Iziaslav Iaroslavich, Iaropolk Iziaslavich (d. 1086), Vsevolod Iaroslavich, and Volodimer Vsevolodich (d. 1125)). Upon seeing the approaching army and its leaders, Oleg remarked to Boris that they could not stand against "chetyr'm" k'niazem'" (four rulers) (PVL, s.a. 1078). Though the ranks of the approaching kniazia were disparate, and included the ruler of Kiev himself, Iziaslav Iaroslavich, this was not an issue for Oleg in his statement. It was the quantity of rulers, and presumably their troops, that were the threat, not the presence of a single overarching ruler, and his subordinates, with their respective forces. This use of the title "kniaz'" is informative for us, reinforcing the meaning of ruler, as well as indicating clearly that there are multiple people bearing that title at the same time. But it also presents a complication, and one of the underlying issues that needs reexamination in regard to the wider world of titulature, as there are four kings (in the suggested emendation to Rusian titulature) that are marching against Oleg Sviatoslavich. The situation in Rus', like that in other places in the medieval European world, was more complicated than a traditional understanding of king as monarch would allow.

The main source for the actions of eleventh and early twelfth century Rus', the PVL, is a problematic one, as it is extant only from the fourteenth century, though it is believed to be a living chronicle by the end of the period under discussion.[56] The lag between the time recorded and the earliest extant copy could have allowed for some change to creep into the text, though such pervasive change seems highly unlikely, as Donald Ostrowski has shown (*Povest' vremennykh let*, Introduction). It is fortunate that we have other sources to check this titulature, internal to Rus'. The first are Rusian charters, *gramoty*, that use the title "kniaz'" for these rulers.[57] There are several examples of this title in those documents, and they exist from the period when they were written, in the case of the two cited, from the twelfth century. There is also a single seal of Iaroslav Volodimerich that bears the title, another contemporary indicator of the use of the title "kniaz'."[58] Several examples of graffiti from the walls of churches, specifically the St. Sophia Churches of Novgorod and Kiev, exist bearing the titles "kniaz'" and "kniaginia" (the feminine form). Though graffiti are difficult to date, we can place them securely in the medieval period more broadly, if not precisely to the eleventh or twelfth century.[59] These sources are especially important for us, as they allow us to corroborate the use of kniaz' as the title of an East Slavic ruler without fear that it is an affectation or invention of a later medieval period.

Though the majority of mentions of the Rusian rulers use the title "kniaz'" in the Rusian sources, there are three additional titles, "*kagan*," "tsar'," and "arkhon," that have been used within Rus', usually as part of appropriating titulature from neighbouring empires. In the eleventh-century encomium to Volodimer, Metropolitan Ilarion (d. pre-1054), the first native metropolitan of Kiev, refers to Volodimer, and once to his son Iaroslav the Wise as "kagan" (Ilarion, pp. 17–26). Though this is an extremely rare mention, it has sparked the imagination of scholars, who have used it to talk about the eastward focus of the Rus', their relations with the steppe, and their ties to the Khazar khaganate, among other topics. Though fascinating, this title is an outlier in Rusian titulature and may have been used by Ilarion for a variety of purposes, including appropriating power and glory from neighbouring, fallen, empires (Hanak, pp. 135–48; Isaievych, p. 220). The other title that appears rarely is "tsar'." A graffito dated to the eleventh century on the wall of the St. Sophia church in Kiev refers to a deceased Rusian ruler as "tsar'."[60] This has been used by some to advance the idea that the Rusians used the title "tsar'" for exceptional rulers of their own, and thus acknowledged "kniaz'" as a lower-ranking title. The more commonly accepted notion, however, is that this reference is a particular type of posthumous honour, elevating the deceased Rusian kniaz' to the ranks of biblical kings for his conduct, rather than for any semblance of earthly power.[61] The rare use of "tsar'" then for a Rusian ruler does not detract from either its description of Byzantine rulers or the primary use of "kniaz'" for the rulers of Rus'. Similarly, it is with a nod to Byzantium that the few internal instances of the title "arkhon" appear within Rus'. Greek language inscriptions became the fashion in the middle of the eleventh century in Rus', and arkhon appeared on the seals of a small number of Rusian rulers, including Vsevolod Iaroslavich and his son Volodimer.[62] It is possible that such titulature was chosen by this subset of the family to highlight their tie with Byzantium, as Vsevolod was married to a woman of the Monomachos clan of Byzantium, and their son Volodimer bore the surname "Monomakh," including in one of his seals.[63] In general, however, such appropriations as these were common in much of Europe. For instance, Byzantine titulature was used to increase rulers' own sense of legitimacy, without creating a physical reliance upon Byzantium (Raffensperger, *Reimagining Europe*, chap. 1). Though these mentions are rare, they point out the place of Rus' in the larger European world, where it had neighbours on both sides that at different times it may have been looking to appease or appropriate. They also point out the complexity of the world of medieval titulature as well as the varying identities that one individual might portray, or attempt to portray, to different facets of the world in which they lived.

The examples shown here, from Latin, German, Old Norse, Greek, and Old East Slavic sources, point to a range of titles for the rulers of Rus'. However, the majority are similar, if not identical, to those used for rulers whose titles are translated into English as "king." Even if we step back further from translation, almost all the titles presented here bear the core meaning of ruler, with no linguistic intimation of subordination. These examples provide a range of information from the sources who knew the Rusian rulers best, their neighbours (who were marital partners, allies, and enemies) as well as themselves. Thus they give us incredibly useful tools to construct our model of what these Rusian rulers should be called.

Notes

[36] "Lamberti Hersfeldensis Annales," ed. V. Cl. Lud. Frid. Hasse, *Monumenta Germaniae Historica Scriptores 5*, ed. George Pertz (Hannover: Impensis Bibliopolii Avlici Hahniani, 1844), s.a. 1075; "Annales Augustani," *Monumenta Germaniae Historica Scriptores 3*, ed. George Pertz (Hannover: Impensis Bibliopolii Avlici Hahniani, 1839), s.a. 1089.

[37] Thietmar of Merseburg, *Chronica*, ed. J. M. Lappenberg, in *Monumenta Germaniae Historica Scriptores 3*, ed. George Pertz (Hannover: Impensis Bibliopolii Aulici Hahniani, 1839; repr., Leipzig: Hiersemann, 1925), bk. 6, chap. 37; bk. 7, chaps. 48, 52; bk. 8, chap. 16.

[38] "Annalista Saxo," *Monumenta Germaniae Historica SS 6*, ed. George Pertz (Hannover: Impensis Bibliopolii Avlici Hahniani, 1844), s.a. 1103.

[39] Bruno of Querfurt, "List Brunona do Henryka II, ok. 1008," in *Monumenta Poloniae Historica*, vol. 1., ed. August Bielowski (Lwow: Nakładem Własnym, 1864), p. 224.

[40] "Wilhelmi Abbatis Genealogia Regum Danorum," in *Scriptores minores historiae danicae medii ævi*, vol. 1, ed. M. C. L. Getz (København: 1917), p. 184.

[41] The whole line is, "Duobus fratribus Russorum regibus de regno contendentibus, alter eorum a consortio regni pulsus, interpellat Heinricum imperatorem, se et regnum Russorum ei submittens, si eius auxilio regno restitueretur." Siegebert of Gembloux, "Chronica Sigeberti Gemblacensis," in *Monumenta Germaniae Historica Scriptores 6*, ed. George Pertz (Hannover: Impensis Bibliopolii Avlici Hahniani, 1844), s.a. 1073.

[42] Admittedly, this depiction is not agreed upon by all, and is not necessarily accurate throughout time. Przemysław Urbańczyk notes the difficulty inherent in the titulature of northern rulers in continental European sources in the early Middle Ages. Specifically, he calls attention to a difference that I would argue is not universally present or accepted in the eleventh and twelfth century, which is the issue of ecclesiastical coronation (or lack thereof) for said northern rulers. Though this topic merits greater discussion elsewhere, the simple fact that the continental European Latin sources referred to many of those non-Christian and early Christian Scandinavian and Slavic rulers as "rex" mitigates against the importance of ecclesiastical coronation in their mindset. Przemysław Urbańczyk, "What Did Early Medieval Authors Know about Structures of Governance and Religion in Northern Central Europe? (A Comment on M. Hardt),"

in *Trade and Communication Networks of the First Millennium AD in the Northern Part of Central Europe: Central Places, Beach Markets, Landing Places and Trading Centres*, ed. Babette Ludowici et al. (Hannover: Niedersächsisches Landesmuseum, 2010), p. 357.

A contrasting example exists as well, from later eastern European history, in which sixteenth-century Muscovy was portrayed by western European writers in their own light. Marshall Poe examined this topic in depth, and pointed out that European theorists used their preexisting ideas about governmental types and "Muscovy was made to fit the theoretical mold." Later writers then used these descriptions to reinforce their own ideas, which were constructed from those same earlier writings, creating what Poe calls a "cycle of reference" that ultimately served to reinforce itself rather than to get closer to an accurate description of Muscovite reality. Marshall T. Poe, *"A People Born to Slavery": Russia in Early Modern European Ethnography, 1476-1748* (Ithaca: Cornell University Press, 2000), pp. 169, 195.

[43] Henricus Lettus, *Heinrici Chronicion Lyvoniae*, published by Wilhelm Arndt (Hannover: Impensis Bibliopolii Hahniani, 1874). These occurrences appear throughout.

[44] A. A. Gorskii, "Dva 'neudobnykh' fakta iz biografii Aleksandra Nevskogo," *Aleksandr Nevskii i istoriia Rossii (Materialy nauchno-prakticheskoi konferentsii 26-28 sentiabria 1995 goda)*, no editor listed (Novgorod: Novgorodskii gosudarstvennyi ob''edinennyi muzei-zapovednik, 1995), pp. 64–65.

[45] For example, "Ic coning Jeretslawe coning Jeretslawen sone." P. V. Petrukhin, "O datirovke spiska A dogovora Smolenska s Rigoi i Gotskim beregom," in *Lingvisticheskoe istochnikovedenie i istoriia russkogo iazyka* (Moscow: Drevlekhranilishche, 2013), p. 168. Thank you to Ann Kleimola for drawing my attention to Pavel Petrukhin's work, and to him for sharing a pdf with me. To add to the complicated nature of this conversation in Russian, Petrukhin translates the phrase quoted as "Ia kniaz' Iaroslav, syn kniazia Iaroslava," utilizing kniaz' as the translation into Russian for "coning."

[46] Karl Ferdinand Werner, "Kingdom and Principality in Twelfth-Century France," in *The Medieval Nobility: Studies on the Ruling Classes of France and Germany from the Sixth to the Twelfth Century*, ed. Timothy Reuter (Amsterdam: North-Holland, 1979), p. 244 n. 3, "Its use was transferred from the emperors of late antiquity to the new kings of the West and from these to non-royal rulers as well." Any ruler, even non-royals, who controlled territory and people could be a princeps.

[47] *Historia Norwegie*, ed. Inger Ekrem and Lars Boje Mortensen, trans. Peter Fisher (Copenhagen: Museum Tusculanum Press, University of Copenhagen, 2003), chap. 9, pp. 80–81. Though the *Historia Norwegie* does also use "rex" for the ruler of Rus', chap. 17, pp. 90–91; chap. 18, pp. 104–05.

[48] Werner, "Kingdom and Property," pp. 243–44.

[49] Bruno of Querfurt, "List Brunona do Henryka II, ok. 1008," p. 224.

[50] *Heimskringla*, 1:230, 232, 251, 252, 291, 338; 2:144, 147, 148, 328, 339, 343, 415; 3:69, 70, 76, 90, 258, 375. *Morkinskinna*, ed. C. R. Unger (Christiana: Det for B. M. Bentzen's Bogtrykkeri, 1867), pp. 1, 2, 3, 4, 6, 15, 16, 17, 169. *Fagrskinna*, ed. C. R. Unger and P. A. Munch (Christiania: Trykt hos P. T. Malling, 1847), pp. 55, 69, 78, 78, 88, 94, 95, 106, 107, 108, 112, 144, 163.

[51] *Heimskringla*, 3:375.

[52] Ihor Ševčenko, "Re-Reading Constantine Porphyrogenitus," in *Byzantine Diplomacy: Papers from the Twenty-Fourth Spring Symposium of Byzantine Studies, Cambridge, March 1990*, ed. Jonathan Shepard and Simon Franklin (Brookfield: Variorum, 1992), pp. 189–94. Jonathan Shepard views the information as largely accurate, if ad hoc. "The Uses of 'History' in Byzantine Diplomacy: Observations and Comparisons," in *Porphyrogenita: Essays on the History and Literature of Byzantium and the Latin East in Honour of Julian Chrysostimides*, ed. J. Chrysostimides et al. (London: Ashgate, 2003), p. 111.

[53] Ioannis Cinnami Epitome rerum ab Ioanne et Alexio Comnenis gestarum. In *Corpus Scriptorum Historiae Byzantinae*, ed. Augustus Meineke (Bonn: Ed. Weberi, 1836), bk. 1, pp. 115, 235; John Scylitzes, *Ioannis Scylitzae Synopsis Historiarum*, ed. Ioannes Thurn (Berlin: de Gruyter, 1973), p. 240; *De cerimoniis aulae Byzantinae*, ed. I. I. Reiske (Bonn: Ed. Weberi, 1829), in Corpus Scriptorum Historiae Byzantinae, ed. B. G. Niebuhrii, vol. 9, p. 594. Jeffrey Featherstone has translated the passages of the *De Cerimoniis* relevant to Ol'ga into English, and he also offers his thoughts on the title "arkhontissa" as the official title for the ruler of Rus'. Jeffrey Featherstone, "Ol'ga's visit to Constantinople," *Harvard Ukrainian Studies* 14 (1990): 293–312. Andrzej Poppe also suggests that the title "velikii kniaz'," usually translated as "grand prince," in the tenth century treaties between Byzantium and Rus' preserved in the PVL is simply a translation of the Greek "megas arkhon," which becomes the title used for the rulers of Rus' later in the twelfth century in Byzantine correspondence. Andrzej Poppe, "On the Title of Grand Prince in the *Tale of Ihor's Campaign*," in *Eucharisterion*, pp. 685–86.

⁵⁴ John Fine notes the use of arkhon for Bulgarian rulers by the Byzantines, even for Symeon, who was often styled "tsar" in Bulgarian. Fine also translates "arkhon" as "prince," in an interesting footnote to the discussion of titulature in this article. John V. A. Fine, Jr., *The Early Medieval Balkans: A Critical Survey from the Sixth to the Late Twelfth Century* (Ann Arbor: University of Michigan Press, 1983), pp. 155–56.

⁵⁵ Jonathan Shepard, "Byzantium and Russia in the Eleventh Century: A Study in Political and Ecclesiastical Relations" (PhD Dissertation, Oxford, 1973), p. 74.

⁵⁶ *The Old Rus' Kievan and Galician-Volhynian Chronicles: The Ostroz'kyj (Xlebnikov) and četvertyns'kyj (Pogodin) Codices*, Omeljan Pritsak, Introduction (Cambridge, MA: Harvard University Press, 1990), p. xx.

⁵⁷ *Gramoty Velikogo Novgoroda i Pskova*, ed. S. N. Valka (Moscow: Akademiia Nauk SSSR, 1949), gramoty 28, 103.

⁵⁸ Simon Franklin, *Writing, Society and Culture in Early Rus', c. 950–1300* (Cambridge: Cambridge University Press, 2002), p. 103 n. 81; V. L. Ianin and P. G. Gaiduko, *Aktovye pechati drevnei rusi X–XV vv.*, vol. 3: *Pechati, zaregistrirovannye v 1970–1996 gg.* (Moscow: Intrada, 1998), pp. 13–14.

⁵⁹ Franklin, *Writing, Society and Culture*, pp. 72–73; S. A. Vysotskii, *Drevne-Russkie nadpisi Sofii Kievskoi, XI–XIV vv.*, vol. 1 (Kiev: Naukova Dumka, 1966), contains a variety of these examples from Kiev, specifically on pp. 18, 35, 42, for example.

⁶⁰ Franklin, *Writing, Society and Culture*, p. 72; Vysotskii, *Drevne-Russkie nadpisi Sofii Kievskoi*, p. 39.

⁶¹ Simon Franklin, "The Empire of the Rhomaioi as Viewed from Kievan Russia: Aspects of Byzantino-Russian Cultural Relations," in *Byzantium—Rus'—Russia: Studies in the Translation of Christian Culture* (Burlington: Ashgate, 2002), pp. 528–29; The title "tsar'" is also dealt with by Tolochko, who notes that there have been a variety of interpretations of the title, including appropriating imperial authority. Tolocho, *kniaz' v drevnei Rusi*, pp. 135–38. Most recently, Walter Hanak discusses the religious use of the title "tsar'" for Volodimer Sviatotoslavich, noting as well the disconnect between that title (which he translates as "Caesar" and not "emperor") and "kniaz'." Hanak, *The Nature and the Image of Princely Power in Kievan Rus'*, pp. 49–50.

⁶² Franklin, *Writing, Society and Culture*, pp. 103–04; *Aktovye pechati drevnei rusi X–XV vv.*, ed. V. L. Ianin, vol. 1: *Pechati X-nachala XIII v.* (Moscow: Nauka, 1970), pp. 15–19.

⁶³ Ianin, *Aktovye pechati drevnei rusi*, seal 25.

Chapter 6

Titles for Other Medieval Rulers in Rusian Sources

The Rusian sources are not particularly forthcoming when it comes to other medieval groups. The PVL tends to focus almost solely on the affairs of the Volodimerovichi, and thus titulature from throughout Europe does not make many appearances. There are, however, a few examples of other rulers discussed in the PVL that deserve mention to contextualize how the Rusians viewed the world, and specifically its rulers, around them.

Polish Rulers

The most often cited Christian neighbour is Poland, even though mention of it is relatively rare as well. As was discussed earlier, the titulature of the Polish ruler was complicated in that he was referred to as "dux" or "rex" depending upon his relationship with the German emperor and/or the papacy. This complication is minimized in the Russian chronicles as the Polish ruler is uniformly referred to as "kniaz'" (for example, PVL, s.a. 996, 1102). The same Slavic word for ruler that the Rusians used for their own rulers applied to the Piast ruler of Poland. The Polish medieval sources were written in Latin, and as such, vernacular writing is extant only from later in history. However, it is understood that while the elite, especially the ecclesiastical elite, wrote in Latin, the language of the majority of the people, including the native-born Piast ruling house, was a Slavic one. Thus, it would not be surprising to find that the Piasts called themselves "książę" (the West Slavic version of "kniaz'"), or their people did, all the while they were labouring to be granted, or to claim, the title of "rex" from the Germans or the papacy. This is important to note not merely as a corollary to Rusian titulature, but as one of the inherent difficulties in studying medieval titulature. The vernacular language was rarely the written language, and utilizing a variety of sources from different places, including where the vernacular was written, helps create a more well-rounded picture of how rulers conceived of themselves in their own ways, as well as in the eyes of their neighbours. It also suggests that a wider investigation into medieval titulature might be necessary.

Hungarian Rulers

Slightly further to their southwest, the Rusians also had increasing dealings with the Árpád ruling family of Hungary in the eleventh and twelfth centuries; their leaders were mentioned in the PVL as well. The few times that the Hungarian ruler appears in Rusian sources he is referred to as "*korol'*," which has since become the modern Russian word for king (Nazarenko, pp. 155–56). The Hungarian sources, like the Polish ones, were written in Latin, and the Árpádian ruler's title was typically an uncomplicated "rex."[64] However, the language they spoke was Magyar, and the word they used for their ruler seems to have been "*király*," which the Byzantine sources record as "*kral*."[65] The word "király," or "kral," has its roots in Magyar relations with Carolingians, perhaps mediated by the Moravian Slavs, and the Germanic name/title Karl (Carolus, Charles).[66] The Rusian sources, then, utilize basically the same word for the Hungarian ruler, merely adding a vowel sound through the process of *polnoglasie* to make it easier to pronounce. As with the Polish title "kniaz'"/"książę," it again appears that the Rusian sources referred to rulers by their internal titles, rather than applying Rusian-based titulature to them. Whether this was an attempt to properly situate those rulers in a regional hierarchy, simple relative accuracy, or a lack of antique examples to draw upon, it provides us an interesting perspective on their relative titulature.

Polovtsian Rulers

The most frequent mentions of non-Rusian rulers in the Rusian sources are those of the Polovtsy. The Polovtsy, nomadic pastoralists, appeared on the steppe south of Rus' in the second half of the eleventh century. They made their presence felt through persistent raiding of the areas bordering the steppe. Their rulers, whose personal names are often given and whose daughters eventually become marital partners, are given the title "kniaz'" in the Rusian chronicles (see PVL, s.a. 1068, 1103 for several instances). The Polovtsy were a Turkic people and so it is highly unlikely that they would have used the title "kniaz'" for themselves. Thus it seems more likely that this is an attribution of Rusian, or more generally Slavic, titulature to the Polovtsy by the Rusian chroniclers. Interestingly, this title is often changed in the secondary sources where the rulers of the Polovtsy are titled "khan" or "chieftain."[67] "Khan" does appear as part of at least one personal name of a Polovtsy ruler listed in the PVL, but nowhere does it appear as a stand-alone title (PVL, s.a. 1094, 1096). Florin Curta has pointed out that, like the issue under discussion here, medieval Bulgarian rulers who are titled "rex" in Latin have their titles changed in English-language secondary sources, in this case to "khan" or "khagan" (Curta, pp. 1–2). As with our main topic here (kniaz'), the use of the title "khan" for the Polovtsian ruler is a modern instrument that creates a perception of the Polovtsy themselves, one that brings to mind the Mongols before all else. Its use, like many of the titles we have seen, deserves another look, so as to create a more accurate and unbiased perception of the medieval past.

Byzantine Rulers

The last of the rulers that the Rusian chronicles discuss are those of the Byzantines, to whom they give the title "tsar'" (see PVL, s.a. 971, 987, 988 for examples). "Tsar'," a Slavonic contraction of the Greek rendering of Caesar, was an appropriate title for the East Roman ruler, though it was not the one that he used himself, preferring the Greek "basileus" (see Franklin, "The Empire of the Rhomaioi"). The Rusians did not just use the title for the emperor in Constantinople, however, but for most any member of the Byzantine nobility that they happened to mention. There are several instances noted by Alexander Kazhdan in which the Rusian chronicle refers to someone with the title *tsarevich*, who is in no known way related to the Byzantine imperial family of the time (Kazhdan, p. 425). This may be due to a phenomenon known as "Byzantine Inflation" in which the Rusian chronicler(s), perhaps because of Byzantine ecclesiastical ties, endeavoured to increase ties with Byzantium in their work (see Raffensperger, *Reimagining Europe*, pp. 54–55). For the purposes of titulature, the title "tsar'" (and its diminutives) is interesting because of its inaccuracy. This was a title not used, largely, by the Byzantines, but it was used by the Rusians to describe them. It was also used by the Rusian chroniclers, and churchmen, when referring to the kings of the Bible, who are regularly referred to as tsars as well (PVL, s.a. 986). Instead of relating "tsar'" to "emperor," as is often done in the secondary literature, it too could be reexamined, especially given its use in relation to the Bible, and could be used as another translation for "king."

In sum, Rusian titulature for their neighbours is a contradiction. In the case of the Poles and the Polovtsy, they used their own, Slavic, title for ruler for the leaders of those groups. For the Poles, this may have translated quite easily into the Polish "książę" and may have been the vernacular word for ruler amongst the West Slavs already. This was certainly not the case among the Turkic Polovtsy, however, and the use of "kniaz'" for those rulers is interesting. Were the Rusian chroniclers ascribing the same characteristics of their own rulers, and the Polish rulers, to the Polovtsian rulers? If so, this would be a leap forward in understanding how the Rusians viewed the Polovtsy. But even if not, it provides another useful piece of information in attempting to decipher the puzzle of medieval titulature. The titulature for the Hungarian rulers was not Rusian, nor was it Magyar, but it was at least what we now believe the Hungarians were using for themselves: an attempt, perhaps, to accurately use the language of titulature from their own territory. For the Byzantines they used one of many titles for a Roman ruler, though not the one the Greek-speaking emperor in Constantinople would have probably preferred. This may be viewed as inconsistency, or it may be viewed along with the plethora of titles in Gregory VII's register as an acknowledgement of the plurality of titles that existed in the medieval world. The examination of these titles, in conjunction with evidence from Latin, Greek, and other sources, helps to create a more complex picture of the reality of medieval eastern European titulature than currently exists today.

Notes

[64] The Hungarian chronicles are uniform for the titulature of their rulers after their conversion to Christianity. For various examples see, "Annales Posonienses," ed. Emericus Madszar, in *Scriptores Rerum Hungaricarum*, ed. Emerus Szentpetery, vol. 1 (Budapest: Academia Litter. Hungarica atque Societate Histo. Hungarica, 1937); "Chronici Hungarici," ed. Alexander Domanovszky, in *Scriptores Rerum Hungaricarum*, ed. Emerus Szentpetery, vol. 1 (Budapest: Academia Litter. Hungarica atque Societate Histo. Hungarica, 1937); *The Hungarian Illuminated Chronicle—Chronica De Gestis Hungarorum*, ed. Dezso Dercesnyi (Budapest: Corvina Press, 1969).

[65] Pál Engel notes both the title of King Stephen as "rex" as well as the Hungarian title. *The Realm of St Stephen: A History of Medieval Hungary, 895–1526*, trans. Tamás Pálosfalvi (London: Tauris, 2005), p. 28; Anna Komnena refers to the Hungarian ruler as "kral." *Alexiad*, bk. 13, p. xii.

[66] Nazarenko, *Drevniaia Rus' na mezhdunarodnykh putiakh*, pp. 155–56. Engel notes it as deriving from Charlemagne: *Realm of St. Stephen*, p. 28. Peter Golden also suggests that it arrived amongst the Slavs through the Polabian Slavs in the ninth century and became "korol." Peter B. Golden, "'Ascent by Scales': The System of Succession in Kievan Rus' in a Eurasian Context," in *States, Societies, Cultures: East and West: Essays in Honor of Jaroslaw Pelenski*, ed. Janusz Duzinkiewicz (New York: Ross, 2004), p. 235.

[67] Franklin and Shepard, *Emergence of Rus*, p. 272. Byzantine secondary sources consistently seem to refer to these rulers as "chieftains." Michael Angold, *The Byzantine Empire, 1025–1204: A Political History* (New York: Longman, 1997), pp. 132–33; Paul Stephenson, *Byzantium's Balkan Frontier: A Political Study of the Northern Balkans, 900–1204* (Cambridge: Cambridge University Press, 2000), p. 101.

Conclusion

Consequences and Resolution

Medieval Europe is growing. The boundaries of this once small world are stretching to the south, east, and north to include the Mediterranean world, Scandinavia, and eastern Europe. Scholars are taking a new look at sources to reexamine how the medieval European world was interconnected in a variety of ways, from marital ties to religion, trade, language, and culture. Part of that movement is an inherent revisionism that requires the casting out of older conceptions of a medieval Europe that had the Rhine as its eastern border, or even a medieval Europe that was merely an expanding Germanic (or Frankish) sphere of influence. What this book proposes is a revision to an ahistorical view of the medieval world. Checking and rechecking translations alongside other historical information allows modern scholars to avoid the presentism of past generations and present a more accurate view of the medieval world.

One simple example of how this change in translation is relevant and what the ramifications might be is in order. In the eleventh century, the Capetian King Henry of France (d. 1060) married Anna (d. 1089), daughter of Iaroslav the Wise of Kiev. This is recorded in a variety of sources and has been discussed frequently in secondary scholarship. However, this information can be presented in different ways that allow the reader to draw different conclusions.

For instance, if we say, King Henry of France married Anna, the daughter of Prince Iaroslav of Kiev, as is often said, one perception is created in the mind of the reader.[68] On the other hand if we say, King Iaroslav of Rus' married his daughter Anna to King Henry of France, another perception entirely is created.[69] In the first statement, Henry is clearly the ranking individual, not simply because of his primary place in the sentence, but because of his title having precedence in the modern mind over "prince" Iaroslav. The marriage is then not one of equals, and not one for a political purpose, but a mere historical vagary or amusement, which may have prompted the distinguished historian of dynastic marriage Constance Bouchard to dismiss this marriage as a novelty (Bouchard, pp. 277, 287). The second formulation places Iaroslav and Henry on an equal plane due to their titulature, and allows for a more nuanced understanding of the marriage, and perhaps its underlying causes. The latter formulation is also accurate in terms of the titulature that the rulers and their contemporaries used, which is an important denominator of historical research.

Neither formulation, however, takes into account the historical realities of their respective geographical positions, for instance the fact that Iaroslav ruled a kingdom that stretched from the Baltic Sea in the north to the Black Sea in the south and from the Western Dvina river to the upper reaches of the Volga and lower Don rivers in the east, while Henry actively controlled the Île de France and little more even in the mid-eleventh century. This characterization is not meant to aggrandize Rus' or diminish France, but simply to show the relative positions in the actual medieval world of the eleventh century and in the minds of modern scholars looking at the eleventh century. The recoil that modern western medievalists feel reading that sentence about respective sizes, and the "but ..." that springs to their mind is the reason that this corrective is so essential. Academics can read scholarship about new approaches to understanding the medieval world, or integrating Rus' or Hungary or elsewhere into the medieval world, but changing minds is a long process.[70] Changing the building blocks of how historians, and people in general, speak about the past, including titulature, is an essential part of making those changes, and one that requires constant work and revision.

The goal of historians is historical accuracy. It has been clear for many years that scholars cannot write or know the "truth" about what happened and why, but we still strive to use a variety of sources, our best interpretations, and the most current scholarship to endeavour to create a medieval world that is as accurate as extant sources and our perceptions can make it. Changing the title of the ruler of Rus' for the eleventh and twelfth centuries may seem like a small thing in the face of daunting demands of scholarship, but it is in the details where the joys and pains of history can be found. "King" in the modern vernacular has connotations of monarch that were not expressed in the medieval formulations of "rex," "konungr," or "kniaz'." However, "king" has been used as the default translation for "rex" and for at least some of those titled "konungr," which has placed those gifted with this translated title on a level higher than the kniazia whose title has been translated as "prince" or "duke." It is clear that there needs to be a wholesale revision of the titulature of medieval rulership to better bring it into line with modern language and medieval reality. This study is merely a small step in that direction in regard to the titulature of the Rusian rulers who were referred to by their contemporaries as "rex" and "konungr," and who thus wrote about the kings, and kingdom, of Rus'.

Notes

[68] Similar sentiments are expressed in a variety of places. I include here two examples of the ways that Rusian rulers are referred to for reference: "in 1051, the aging Henry married Anna of Russia, the daughter of Grand Duke Yaroslav of Kiev." Constance B. Bouchard, "Consanguinity and Noble Marriages in the Tenth and Eleventh Centuries," *Speculum* 56 (1981): 277. "Sophia, daughter of Prince Volodar of Novgorod and his Swedish wife, Richeza, married Waldemar I the Great" Inge Skovgaard-Petersen (in collaboration with Nanna Damsholt). "Queenship in Medieval Denmark," in *Medieval Queenship*, ed. John Carmi Parsons (Gloucestershire: Sutton, 1994), p. 41.

[69] Of course, the most accurate statement would be something along the lines of Iaroslav, king of the Rusians, married his daughter Anna, to Henry, king of the Franks, though this is not the place to discuss that particular vagary of titulature.

[70] There are a lot of very good scholars working on expanding our perceptions of what the medieval world was, but the diverse work of Ildar Garipzanov, especially his emphasis on translating his edited collections into English to reach a wider audience, I find especially worthwhile examples. *Historical Narratives and Christian Identity on a European Periphery: Early History Writing in Northern, East-Central, and Eastern Europe (c. 1070–1200)*, ed. Ildar Garipzanov (Turnhout: Brepols, 2011); *Saints and their Lives on the Periphery Veneration of Saints in Scandinavia and Eastern Europe (c. 1000–1200)*, ed. Ildar Garipzanov and Haki Thor Antonsson (Turnhout: Brepols, 2010); *Franks, Northmen, and Slavs: Identities and State Formation in Early Medieval Europe*, ed. Ildar Garipzanov, Patrick Geary, and Przemyslaw Urbanczyk (Turnhout: Brepols, 2008).

Further Reading

Primary Sources

Comnena, Anna. *The Alexiad of Anna Comnena*. Translated by E. R. A. Sewter. New York: Penguin Books, 1969.

> The only female Byzantine historian, Comnena is a vital source for medieval and Byzantine history.

Cosmas of Prague. *The Chronicle of the Czechs by Cosmas of Prague*. Translated by Lisa Wolverton. Washington, DC: Catholic University of America Press, 2009.

> Cosmas of Prague provides lucid coverage of a large swath of medieval Europe, focused mostly on Bohemia, Moravia, and the German empire.

Fletcher, Giles. "Of the Russe Commonwealth." In *Rude and Barbarous Kingdom: Russia in the Accounts of Sixteenth-Century English Voyagers*, edited by Lloyd E. Berry and Robert O. Crummey. Madison: University of Wisconsin Press, 1968.

> An Englishman's guide to Muscovy and some of the first early modern contacts between western and eastern Europe.

Gesta Principum Polonorum: The Deeds of the Princes of the Poles. Edited and translated by Paul W. Knoll and Frank Schaer. New York: Central European University Press, 2003.

> One of the earliest narrative sources for the history of Poland,

focused mainly on the work of the family of Miesko known as the Piasts.

Henricus Lettus. *The Chronicle of Henry of Livonia*. Translated by James A. Brundage. New York: Columbia University Press, 2003.

> An account of the Baltic crusades, though Henry would not call them that himself. They are an important source for the interactions of Germans, Swedes, Rusians, and Baltic peoples in the thirteenth century.

The Hungarian Illuminated Chronicle—Chronica De Gestis Hungarorum. Edited by Dezso Dercesnyi. Budapest: Corvina Press, 1969.

> One of the earliest narrative sources for the history of Hungary.

Ilarion. "Encomium to Volodimer." In *Sermons and Rhetoric of Kievan Rus'*, translated by Simon Franklin, pp. 17–26. Cambridge, MA: Harvard University Press, 1991.

> Ilarion is the first Rusian to be named Metropolitan of Kiev. This encomium is an early native testament for both Volodimer and Iaroslav, his son.

Ottonian Germany: The "Chronicon" of Thietmar of Merseburg. Translated by David A. Warner. Manchester: Manchester University Press, 2001.

> Thietmar's chronicle covers much more than the German Empire, including events in Poland and Rus', especially the succession struggle after the death of Volodimer.

The Povest' vremennykh let: An Interlinear Collation and Paradosis. Compiled and edited by Donald Ostrowski, with David Birnbaum and Horace G. Lunt. Cambridge, MA: Harvard University Press, 2004.

> The earliest, and only in many cases, chronicle source for Rusian history. Though problematic due to its late date, it is the only source we have for many events in eleventh-century Rus'.

The Russian Primary Chronicle: Laurentian Text. Edited and translated by Samuel Hazzard Cross and Olgerd P. Sherbowitz-Wetzor. Cambridge, MA: Medieval Academy of America, 1953.

> The English-language translation of the Povest' vremennykh let.

Sturluson, Snorri. *Heimskringla: History of the Kings of Norway.* Translated by Lee M. Hollander. Austin: University of Texas Press, 1964.

> A thirteenth-century history of the kings of Norway detailing not only their activities at home, but their travels and interactions with people throughout Europe.

Secondary Sources

Abels, Richard. "The Historiography of a Construct: 'Feudalism' and the Medieval Historian." *History Compass* 7 (2009): 1008–31.

> A historiographical review of one of the most interesting debates in modern medieval studies—the development of the idea of feudalism.

Althoff, Gerd. *Otto III.* Translated by Phyllis G. Jestice. University Park: Pennsylvania State University Press, 2003.

> Otto III is a fascinating emperor who was both German and Byzantine, with all of the accompanying advantages and disadvantages that brings to bear.

Andrusiak, Mykola and A. Mykytiak. "Kings of Kiev and Galicia: On the Occassion of the 700th Anniversary of the Coronation of Danilo Romanovich." *Slavonic and East European Review* 33 (1955): 342–49.

> An example of the Ukrainian historiography that deals with the idea of a "king" of Rus'.

Angold, Michael. *The Byzantine Empire, 1025-1204: A Political History*. New York: Longman, 1997.

A reliable and readable textbook of Byzantine political history.

Berend, Nora, Przemysław Urbańczyk, and Przemysław Wiszewski. *Central Europe in the High Middle Ages: Bohemia, Hungary and Poland c. 900–c. 1300*. Cambridge: Cambridge University Press, 2013.

An excellent English-language history of medieval Poland, Bohemia and Hungary that covers the political, social, and cultural histories of each of those areas.

Bernhardt, John W. *Itinerant Kingship and Royal Monasteries in Early Medieval Germany, c. 936–1075*. Cambridge: Cambridge University Press, 1993.

Bernhardt makes an important contribution about the itinerant nature of medieval kingship that is applicable beyond the boundaries of the German Empire.

Bouchard, Constance B. "Consanguinity and Noble Marriages in the Tenth and Eleventh Centuries." *Speculum* 56 (1981): 268–87.

A classic article on the issues related to dynastic marriage in medieval Europe.

Byrne, F. J. *Irish Kings and High-kings*. London: Batsford, 1973.

The classic study of Irish rulership.

Christiansen, Eric. *Norsemen in the Viking Age*. Oxford: Blackwell, 2002.

A good, reliable textbook study of Scandinavian history in the Viking period. Christiansen also emphasizes the interconnectivity promoted by the Viking Age.

Cowdrey, H. E. J. *Pope Gregory VII 1073–1085*. Oxford: Clarendon Press, 1998.

Cowdrey's analysis of the pontificate of Gregory VII is thorough and grounded in his work with Pope Gregory's letters.

Curta, Florin. "Qagan, Khan, or King? Power in Early Medieval Bulgaria (Seventh to Ninth Centuries)." *Viator* 37 (2006): 1–31.

> Curta brings his own challenge of titulature, this time in southeastern Europe to the rulers of Bulgaria.

Dimnik, Martin. *The Dynasty of Chernigov 1054–1146.* Toronto: Pontifical Institute of Mediaeval Studies, 1994.

> In this first book of a duology, Dimnik attempts to reconstruct the history of Chernigov, from the point of view of its rulers, the Sviatoslavichi.

——. "The Title 'Grand Prince' in Kievan Rus'." *Mediaeval Studies* 66 (2004): 253–312.

> Dimnik examines the title "grand prince" in some detail, both for practical and spiritual relations within Rus'.

Doherty, Charles. "Kingship in Early Ireland." In *The Kingship and Landscape of Tara*, edited by Edel Bhreathnach, pp. 1–31. Dublin: Four Courts, 2005.

> An updated study on Irish kingship, with a focus on kings and their people.

Engel, Pál. *The Realm of St Stephen: A History of Medieval Hungary, 895–1526.* Translated by Tamás Pálosfalvi. London: Tauris, 2005.

> A solid textbook survey of Hungarian medieval history with a focus on social, economic, and cultural history.

Fine, John V. A. *The Early Medieval Balkans: A Critical Survey from the Sixth to the Late Twelfth Century.* Ann Arbor: University of Michigan Press, 1983.

> The first book of a duology providing the most comprehensive political history of the medieval Balkans in English.

Forte, Angelo, Richard Oram, and Frederik Pedersen. *Viking Empires*. Cambridge: Cambridge University Press, 2005.

> A textbook study of the Viking world from the perspective of the idea of Vikings as rulers not just raiders throughout northern Europe.

Franklin, Simon. "The Empire of the Rhomaioi as Viewed from Kievan Russia: Aspects of Byzantino-Russian Cultural Relations." In *Byzantium—Rus'—Russia: Studies in the Translation of Christian Culture*, pp. 507–37. Burlington: Ashgate, 2002.

> Franklin analyzes the relationship between Rus' and Byzantium, with a focus on Rusian perceptions of Byzantium.

———. *Writing, Society and Culture in Early Rus', c. 950–1300*. Cambridge: Cambridge University Press, 2002.

> A comprehensive study of writing and written culture in Rus', including all of the early extant examples and what they mean for Rusian cultural history.

Franklin, Simon and Jonathan Shepard. *The Emergence of Rus, 750–1200*. New York: Longman, 1996.

> The now classic textbook of Rusian history.

Franks, Northmen, and Slavs: Identities and State Formation in Early Medieval Europe. Edited by Ildar H. Garipzanov, Patrick J. Geary, and Przemysław Urbańczyk. Turnhout: Brepols, 2008.

> A compendium of articles that deal with the important concepts of identity and state formation during a formative period of medieval European history.

Geary, Patrick J. *The Myth of Nations: The Medieval Origins of Europe*. Princeton: Princeton University Press, 2002.

> This is an easy access point to Geary's broader theme of the modern use and construction of the medieval past.

Golden, Peter B. "'Ascent by Scales': The System of Succession in Kievan Rus' in a Eurasian Context." In *States, Societies, Cultures: East and West: Essays in Honor of Jaroslaw Pelenski*, edited by Janusz Duzinkiewicz, pp. 229–58. New York: Ross, 2004.

> Golden brings a Turkic focus to his study of the system of succession in Rus'.

Hanak, Walter K. *The Nature and the Image of Princely Power in Kievan Rus', 980–1054*. Leiden: Brill, 2013.

> Hanak collects a broad variety of primary sources from multiple languages to attempt a new analysis of the early rulers of Rus'.

Historical Narratives and Christian Identity on a European Periphery: Early History Writing in Northern, East-Central, and Eastern Europe (c. 1070–1200). Edited by Ildar Garipzanov. Turnhout: Brepols, 2011.

> A collection of multiple studies on the creation of identity via narrative sources in medieval Europe, especially in Scandinavia and eastern Europe.

Isaievych, Iaroslav. "On the Titulature of Rulers in Eastern Europe." *Journal of Ukrainian Studies* 29 (2004): 219–44.

> Isaievych offers an analysis of titulature of rulers, largely in Rus'.

Jackson, Peter. *The Mongols and the West, 1221–1410*. Harlow: Pearson, 2005.

> The image of the Mongols in medieval Europe largely focuses on eastern Europe in the 1240s, but Jackson demonstrates the deeper interactions between Christian medieval Europe and the Mongol world.

Kaldellis, Anthony. *The Byzantine Republic: People and Power in New Rome*. Cambridge, MA: Harvard University Press, 2015.

> A novel approach to Byzantine governance, making the argu-

ment that Byzantium was a republic and continuous in that way with Rome from the Ancient world.

——. *Hellenism in Byzantium: The Transformations of Greek Identity and the Reception of the Classical Tradition.* Cambridge: Cambridge University Press, 2007.
> Kaldellis makes a cogent argument for the Greek background of Byzantium and its uses there, as well as a critique of Obolensky and the Byzantine Commonwealth.

Kazhdan, Alexander. "Rus'-Byzantine Princely Marriages in the Eleventh and Twelfth Centuries." *Harvard Ukrainian Studies*, 12/13 (1988/89): 414–29.
> Kazhdan examines the primary source evidence for these marriages and demonstrates that many of the marriages listed in the scholarship are not borne out by primary source evidence.

Kollman, Nancy Shields. "Collateral Succession in Kievan Rus'." *Harvard Ukrainian Studies* 14 (1990): 377–87.
> One of the main examples of an attempt to demonstrate a "system" for Rusian succession to the various thrones and cities.

Leyser, Karl. *Medieval Germany and its Neighbours, 900–1250.* London: Hambledon, 1982.
> The major German historian evaluates the political relationships between the German Empire and its closest neighbours, though it does not deal with the Slavic world.

Martin, Janet. *Medieval Russia, 980–1584.* 2nd ed. Cambridge: Cambridge University Press, 2007.
> The best textbook treatment of medieval Russia, continuous from Kievan Rus' through Muscovy.

Mikhailova, Yulia. *Property, Power, and Authority in Rus' and Latin Europe, ca. 1000–1236.* Michigan: ARC-Humanities Press, forthcoming.
> A unique treatment of Normandy and Rus' as examples of

rule, via close reading of primary sources, in medieval Europe.

Nazarenko, A. V. *Drevniaia Rus' na mezhdunarodnykh puti-akh: Mezhditsiplinarnye ocherki kul'turnykh, torgovykh, politicheskikh sviazei IX–XII vekov.* Moscow: Iazyki Russkoi Kul'tury, 2001.

A series of studies by a major Russian scholar of this period, dealing with specific examples of Rusian relations with the rest of medieval Europe.

Ostrowski, Donald. "Systems of Succession in Rus' and Steppe Societies." *Ruthenica* 11 (2012): 31–33.

A new and compelling analysis of the various methods by which Rusian rulers claimed and held power in Rus'.

Petrukhin, P. V. "O datirovke spiska a dogovora Smolenska s Rigoi i Gotskim beregom." In *Lingvisticheskoe istochnikovedenie i istoriia russkogo iazyka.* Edited by A. M. Moldovan. Moscow: Drevlekhranilishche, 2013.

A publication of a treaty between Smolensk and Riga, covering the specifics of the date of this treaty.

Poppe, Andrzej. "Words that Serve the Authority: On the Title of 'Grand Prince' in Kievan Rus'." In *Christian Russia in the Making*, pp. 159–91. Aldershot: Ashgate, 2007.

Another treatment of the titulature of "grand prince," which includes a refutation of Dimnik's article on the subject.

Raffensperger, Christian. *Reimagining Europe: Kievan Rus' in the Medieval World.* Cambridge, MA: Harvard University Press, 2012.

An ambitious study of the place of Kievan Rus' in Europe covering dynastic marriage, religion, and trade as well as the concept of the Byzantine Ideal.

————. *Ties of Kinship: Genealogy and Dynastic Marriage in Kyivan Rus'*. Cambridge, MA: Harvard Ukrainian Research Institute, 2016.

> A new study of the dynastic marriages of the Rusian royal family, and analysis of those marriages with the rest of medieval Europe.

Reynolds, Susan. *Fiefs and Vassals: The Medieval Evidence Reinterpreted*. Oxford: Clarendon Press, 1996.

> Reynolds's argument against the older interpretation of feudalism takes historians back to the primary sources—what they say and what they mean.

Robinson, I. S. *Henry IV of Germany, 1056–1106*. Cambridge: Cambridge University Press, 1999.

> A comprehensive study of this incredibly important ruler of the German Empire and the events of his reign.

Saints and their Lives on the Periphery: Veneration of Saints in Scandinavia and Eastern Europe (c. 1000–1200). Edited by Ildar Garipzanov and Haki Thor Antonsson. Turnhout: Brepols, 2010.

> A collection of articles attempting to integrate Scandinavian and eastern European saints and their context into the larger medieval world.

Sawyer, Birgit and Peter. *Medieval Scandinavia: From Conversion to Reformation, circa 800–1500*. Minneapolis: University of Minnesota Press, 1993.

> A classic textbook treatment of Scandinavia that moves beyond the Scandinavians as Vikings.

Ševčenko, Ihor. "Re-Reading Constantine Porphyrogenitus." In *Byzantine Diplomacy: Papers from the Twenty-Fourth Spring Symposium of Byzantine Studies, Cambridge, March 1990*, edited by Jonathan Shepard and

Simon Franklin, pp. 167–96. Brookfield: Variorum, 1992.

A fascinating rethinking of the De Administrando Imperio that calls into question the veracity of this tenth-century document.

Soloviev, A. V. "'Reges' et 'Regnum Russiae' au Moyen Âge." *Byzantion* 36 (1966): 144–73.

One of the earliest twentieth-century studies dealing with titulature in Rus'. It collects in one place many of the Latin sources that reference the Rusian ruler's title as "rex."

Stephenson, Paul. *Byzantium's Balkan Frontier: A Political Study of the Northern Balkans, 900–1204*. Cambridge: Cambridge University Press, 2000.

An excellent analysis of the political relationships of the medieval Balkans, specifically focused upon the Byzantines.

Tolocho, A. P. *Kniaz' v drevnei Rusi: Vlast', sobstvennost', ideologiia*. Kiev: Naukova Dumka, 1992.

A respected Ukrainian scholar tackles the issue of what a kniaz' was, his roles and functions in medieval Rus'.

Wickham, Chris. *Framing the Early Middle Ages: Europe and the Mediterranean, 400–800*. Oxford: Oxford University Press, 2005.

An ambitious attempt to lay out a new framework for discussing the Middle Ages, ideally moving beyond a western European focus.

Winroth, Anders. *The Conversion of Scandinavia: Vikings, Merchants, and Missionaries in the Remaking of Northern Europe*. New Haven: Yale University Press, 2012.

A new attempt at a treatment of Scandinavian conversion that puts it into a much broader context of medieval European practice.

Wolff, Larry. *Inventing Eastern Europe: The Map of Civilization on the Mind of the Enlightenment.* Stanford: Stanford University Press, 1994.

A now classic argument that Eastern Europe as a discursive category is created in the eighteenth century.